A Pilgrim's Way

A Pilgrim's Way

WALTER C. RIGHTER

ALFRED A. KNOPF NEW YORK 1998

THIS IS A BORZOI BOOK
PUBLISHED BY ALFRED A. KNOPF, INC.

Library of Congress Cataloging-in-Publication Data
Righter, Walter C.
    A pilgrim's way / Walter C. Righter.
        p.   cm.
    ISBN 0-679-45442-X.—ISBN 0-679-77655-9 (pbk.)
    1. Righter, Walter C.
    2. Ordination of gays—Episcopal Church.
    3. Homosexuality—Religious aspects—Episcopal Church.
    4. Episcopal Church. Diocese of Newark—Biography.
    5. Episcopal Church—Bishops—Biography.
    I. Title.
    BX5995.R49A3   1998
    283'.092
    [B]—dc21   97-49461
                    CIP

Manufactured in the United States of America

First Edition

For Nancy
lover, wife, and friend

Contents

Acknowledgments

Throughout the period from January 1995 to July 1997, there is one person who gave of time, energy, affection, and love in a way I have never experienced before—my wife, Nancy. While holding down a full-time job as a clinical social worker, she managed two additional full-time jobs (if not in fact, at least in substance). Publicity, correspondence, telephone calls, and lack of money all demanded a home office of sorts, to which my work habits never gave much order. Nancy saw to it each day that order was imposed and the constant demands of others were being met. When newspapers and photographers and TV networks all wanted to arrive on the same day, she had our house in "apple-pie order" for the invasion. Many evenings, after a full day's work, she would work on the word processor or on the phone till past midnight. When I had to travel, she arranged her schedule to travel with me. When I occasionally got discouraged at the snail-like speed with which my case proceeded, she transformed herself from office manager/secretary to loving and supportive wife.

When I got too serious or occasionally pompous, she inserted a sense of humor that put a pin in my hot-air balloons. As each day came to an end, I felt an enormous sense of peace and love between us. Together, we made of a nasty situation an opportunity for mission in the best sense of that Christian idea. Together, we felt privileged. Our relationship deepened profoundly because of the pressures placed upon us in this period in our lives. We made some history together. For her presence in my life and her love and support, I am grateful.

There were literally thousands of people who communicated messages of support during the period of my attempted heresy trial. To all of those people, I am profoundly appreciative for their willingness to express their own personal convictions to me on behalf of gay and lesbian persons and their friends and families.

I am additionally grateful to Nancy's children, David, and his wife, Maryrose, and Kathy; to my children, Richard, and his wife, Shirley, and Becky and her companion, Don; to my brother, Richard, and his wife, Jean, and their family. All stayed close to us as the process unfolded. Sometimes they shared our laughter, at other times our anger, at still other times our astonishment and our hope.

Five people especially deserve a word of gratitude. Primary among them is Michael Rehill, chancellor of the Diocese of Newark, lawyer, and churchman extraordinaire. Brilliant at history, theology, and law, he provided a constant and cogent defense as well as being a person I could trust implicitly. His sense of humor was both incisive and leprechaunish!

Louie Crew, founder of Integrity, and faithful friend. He and his partner, Ernest Clay, always represented the unconditional love and acceptance of the gay and lesbian community for us, showing us an icon of the church we hope for.

Barry Stopfel and his partner, Will Leckie, were by our

side throughout the presentment. Under intense pressure each day because of the charges against me and their attendant publicity, they lived out their lives as rector and spouse at St. George's, Maplewood, New Jersey, with courage, dignity, and a sense of humor. They were available to both of us at all times, supporting us, and sometimes cursing with us. All of these men made clear for us what it is to have friends in Christ Jesus.

My endless thanks to my agent, Phillipa Brophy, and her assistants from Sterling Lord Literistic, for guiding me through a complex system. To Jeanne Braham and to my editor, Jane Garrett, and the many at Knopf, especially Kevin Bourke, Carol Edwards, Robert Olsson, Claire Bradley, Archie Ferguson, and Jill Morrison, who gave form and order to my work, my eternal thanks.

Friends from years past, who also happened to be clergy, were like comfortable old clothes that you wear and feel secure in no matter how bad the storms are around you. Steve Snider, whom I ordained almost twenty-five years ago in Iowa, was always there for both of us. When the locus of the pretrial hearings was shifted to Wilmington, he met our planes, transported us to the places we needed to go, and called on the phone frequently to make sure we were holding together. His experience with the police in Iowa made him ready and able to guard both of us if it became necessary. The people of his fine parish in a suburb of Philadelphia, Holy Apostles, Wynnewood, tolerated his absence during those days when he was caring for us, because they had a sense of the greater purpose of the church and their place in it.

Jack Spong, the Bishop of Newark, who befriended me in the House of Bishops early on in our ministry as bishops, not only was personally supportive but also saw to it that the Diocese of Newark was a support community, as well. His leadership in that diocese is magnificent. It was apparent in the way in which he enabled and encouraged his chancellor to be my attorney, his suffragan, Jack McKelvey, to be my chaplain in Wilmington, Delaware, and Jack Croneberger, rector of the Church of the Atonement in Tenafly, New Jersey, and Rudy Knolker, lay person and founding member of Oasis, to be cochairs of the drive to raise funds for my defense. When Barbara Lescota volunteered, as a member of the Diocesan Treasurer John Zinn's staff, to account for receipts and expenditures of the Righter Defense Fund, he encouraged and approved that as well. It showed even more profoundly in the way in which Jack and his wife, Chris, invited us to the diocese for several different kinds of occasions, when we experienced their warmth and welcome.

Attending the House of Bishops was never an easy task for me. When faced with the accusation of heresy, attendance became a complicated event, like walking through a minefield. Several times, the chaplain to the House of Bishops, Martin Smith, superior of the Society of St. John the Evangelist, came to my aid and helped me center my thoughts as I tried gamely to participate in the life of the House of Bishops while staying clearly in touch with God.

The people of the Monadnock region of southwestern New Hampshire have made us glad to claim them as friends and the area as "home." They have given us understanding, support, encouragement and have helped us to maintain a real quality of life. I am grateful to all who have helped Nancy and me.

My thanks also go to all those good-spirited, thoughtful, and kind people who perceived a legal process as a grossly inadequate way for the Christian church to shape any part of its social ethic, especially its sexual ethic. The debate continues now and the process of shaping that ethic goes on. It is a significant process and it will, I am sure, produce a significant social contract for use in the new millennium. I am, finally, grateful to God for giving me a small part in the beginning of that process. The future, while uncertain, is filled with excitement, as long as we approach it with courage.

Walter C. Righter
November 1997

A Pilgrim's Way

CHAPTER 1

A Pilgrim's Way

THERE IS NO CORE DOCTRINE prohibiting the ordination of a noncelibate homosexual person living in a faithful and committed sexual relationship with a person of the same sex. There is no discipline of the church prohibiting the ordination of a noncelibate person living in a committed relationship with a person of the same sex." The ninth Bishop of Delaware, the Rt. Rev. C. Cabell Tennis, spoke those words from the chancel steps of his neo-Gothic cathedral, situated in Wilmington, the see of his diocese. The statement, which followed earlier pretrial hearings in Hartford and Wilmington, electrified the life of the Episcopal church and, by extension, the Anglican Communion.

It was May of 1996. Spring had come and its freshness was in the air. After hearing the decision, there were those who felt spring had arrived in the life of the church, as well. New life, new beauty, new growth, new vigor, new light. I was sitting in the front pew of the cathedral with my wife, Nancy, and my attorney, Michael Rehill. Nancy and I were holding

hands tightly. My anxiety about the whole day combined sus-
pense, joy, and tension as the feelings of the last fifteen months
crystallized in the few seconds before "Cabby" Tennis spoke.
Is this what it all comes to? I thought. Forty-four years of
faithful service as a priest and a bishop ends in a court hearing? Still, I was hopeful about the result.

Nancy and I had talked about possible outcomes.
What if the court said I had violated a core doctrine? Should I
renounce my orders before we went to trial and have done
with it? Did I really want to remain in Holy Orders in a
church that would bow to the pressure of a mean-spirited
minority and convict me of heresy for ordaining a person as
qualified as Barry Stopfel? Each time we had that discussion,
we agreed it was better for everyone if I simply allowed the
situation to unfold. The gay and lesbian community and particularly the witness the church is commissioned to make
would be served only if I carried out my responsibility to God
as a bishop by sticking to the case and pleading my innocence.

My concern embraced Barry Stopfel and Will Leckie,
as well as the members of the gay and lesbian community who
had supported me so completely for fifteen months. Once
I had been accused, tremendous energy came our way from
supporters we had never met. Many of those supporters,
including Barry and Will, were in the cathedral to hear Cabby
Tennis's words. Fifteen minutes into Bishop Tennis's statement, Michael leaned over to Nancy and said, "My God, they
bought my whole argument." I thought, Wow! It's been
worth it. When Bishop Tennis finished his statement, Michael and I shared a strong handshake. I wanted to stand up
and cheer. But I sat quietly and waited for statements by three
other bishops to come to an end. One of the bishops, Donis
Patterson, retired Bishop of Dallas, was in accord with the
court's decision but he needed to caution us to take one an-

other to God in prayer, instead of to court. The second bishop, Roger White, of Milwaukee, Wisconsin, was in accord with the court's decision, but he needed to tell everyone he hoped no more of these ordinations would occur until the church had made an official decision at its General Convention to ordain gays and lesbians who, like Barry Stopfel, were in committed relationships. The third bishop, Andy Fairfield of North Dakota, was the sole dissenter. He argued that not only should gays and lesbians be excluded from ordination but that, in effect, women were incomplete without men, yoking the ordination of women to the issue of full enfranchisement of gays and lesbians. I reacted strongly, and Nancy's reaction was intense. She saw Andy's statement as being painfully inappropriate in a consecrated space and as a personal violation of human dignity.

Bishop Tennis spoke his words on behalf of the eight other bishops who, with him, composed the Court for the Trial of a Bishop. One of those bishops, Fred Borsch, Bishop of Los Angeles, was not present. He did not issue any public statement about his reason for not being present. We were told he had recused himself. Those who knew him guessed, quite reasonably, that he did not want the recent ordination of a gay man in his diocese to affect the way people viewed the court's decision.

The presentment—the accusation—brought against me in 1995 caught people by surprise. In the world of diplomacy and statecraft, such an accusation would be called an attempted "coup d'état." In the ecclesiastical world of the Episcopal Church, it is called a "presentment." Ten bishops, colleagues of mine in the church's House of Bishops, agreed to present—accuse—me of teaching and acting in a way contrary to the doctrine of the Episcopal Church and of violating my ordination vows. The precipitating reason was my decision to ordain to the diaconate Barry Stopfel, a Candidate for Holy Orders in the Episcopal Diocese of Newark. He was living in a committed, faithful, monogamous relationship with Will Leckie. Thus began the long and tedious process leading to an ecclesiastical trial.

The word *heresy* is shorthand for the accusation. People schooled in the church's history were quick to point out that a heresy trial had happened only once before in the history of the Episcopal church in the United States, making my case the second in slightly more than two hundred years! In both instances, the accused bishops were retired. (I retired in January 1989, prior to the long process of the trial.) Although attempts had been made through the years to try active bishops, they had evaded the process successfully. It seems one is more vulnerable when retired.

How had I found myself in this position, of being plucked out of the panorama of social and religious history to be tried for heresy? In his well-known book *The Making of the President 1964*, Theodore White created a lyrical description of how social history unfolds, and this description can also serve as a metaphor for church history and my understanding of my own journey. White described an "immense journey . . . an enormous trek . . . of people, some weary, some gay [happy], some infuriated by the slowness of the pace, and others who insist the journey pause because the pace is too fast." This is the way the pilgrim people who follow the ways of God might be described as they move through history. I found the pilgrim's way gradually but not, by any stretch of the imagination, easily.

I WAS BORN IN 1923 in Hahneman Hospital, in Philadelphia, Pennsylvania, amid a controversy of some years standing over homeopathic, or allopathic, medicine. Hahneman was a homeopathic hospital, and our family doctor was a homeopathic practitioner. My grandfather had equipped our doctor's office for him when he graduated from medical school. In return, he had agreed to provide free medical care to my grandfather and members of his family. Hence, I was a "freebie."

The Righter family had been in Philadelphia since 1690, when Peter Righter arrived from Halle, Germany. He settled initially in a section of Philadelphia called Wissahickon. There he became a member of a Protestant religious community named Monks of the Wissahickon. The monks and the area—named for the creek that runs through Fairmount Park, one of the largest municipal parks in the United States—were the precursors of many religious communities that arose in the centuries afterward: Ephrata, Pennsylvania; New Harmony, Indiana; Amana, Iowa; and several other places. The Wissahickon community was given to contemplative life. One can still visit one of the cells where a monk sat in isolation most of the day, emerging only for some communal duties before the day ended. Peter Righter left that community eventually, married, continued to live nearby, and, along with his wife, raised a family of many children. Righter Street still exists in the area where he once lived. Since that time, generation after generation of my family have been craftsmen and farmers in the area. In lower Merion, a Philadelphia suburb, one can travel on Righter's Mill Road and Righter's Ferry Road, each named for successive generations that founded and operated a ferry across the Schuylkill River and a grain mill. My brother and I found the ruins of John Righter's mill, and to this day we each take great delight in having a brick from those ruins on the hearth in each of our homes.

I was the first person in my family, in the 233 years following the arrival of Peter Righter, to be born in a hospital. My paternal relatives were Episcopalians. Because my maternal relatives were Presbyterians, I was baptized by a Presbyterian minister and went to Sunday school until I was fourteen years of age in the church where I was baptized. The neighborhood I lived in as a child had gas streetlights. I can remember looking out our living room windows each evening and watching the lamplighter climb his ladder and light each streetlight in our neighborhood. The Industrial Revolution and the scientific and medical advances it spawned gave birth, about the time I was born, to new kinds of hospitals and uses for them, and, eventually, electric lights for our streets. However, other profoundly human concerns, that would one day tear the church apart, did not move with the same speed or technological advance.

When I was fourteen years old, a friend and I decided to play hooky from school and go to a burlesque theater in Philadelphia. The theater, known as the Trocadero, was old and creaky, with plain wooden benches in the balcony. We sat in the balcony, feeling sneaky and bold at the same time. The dancing, even for our naïve fourteen-year-old minds, was what we considered corny and somewhat crude. It evoked raucous cheers from all over the theater. My friend and I giggled nervously. We went back to school the next day with our education about life advanced slightly and with lots to brag about to our peers. A week went by and my friend and I felt safe. Then, at supper one evening, my mother said, "Graham's mother called. She said you and Graham played hooky and went to the Trocadero burlesque show. Is that true?" As my face grew beet red, my younger brother, who was seven years old, giggled. He did not know what the Trocadero or burlesque was, but he was enjoying my distress. As my grandmother headed for the kitchen in a hurry, Father and Mother tried in a somewhat stilted and embarrassed way to have a conversation with me about *sex*. My father even added, "If you want to see a show like that, I'll be glad to take you to one." One thing was clear: The local priest didn't occur to my parents as an appropriate resource, even though my father was a vestryman at our parish. So we all stumbled through my trip to the Trocadero and my first major crisis as a teenager in search of self, with only our inner resources to count on. To be twentieth-century people in the 1930s meant we could benefit from medical and scientific breakthroughs, but we had to struggle on our own with issues of human development. Later that evening, I could hear my parents expressing their uncertainty about our discussions, wondering if they had handled the conversation with me appropriately.

Sexuality was a hard topic to discuss. In the 1930s, homosexuality was hardly talked about in our family at all. I had heard the word used to describe a man who had been married to my aunt for a brief time, and there was nothing judgmental in what I was told. Instead, I felt sadness surround that issue, and later on in life I was to discover more about that story. I put the visit to the Trocadero behind me quickly and got on with important teenage activities. There was a driver's license to get, big bands to dance to, country roads to park on and then neck, and high school to graduate from. My social life was hectic and delightful, but I was naïve about things sexual. My parents aided and abetted that social life by permitting me to use their car frequently and encouraging me to participate in social activities, especially after we moved to Pittsburgh in 1940. They did little or nothing about my sexual education. My friends and I used to chuckle about the inept efforts of parents as they tried to tell their children about the birds and the bees, yet somehow, these parents and their children all survived this.

The picture changed dramatically when Europe went

to war in 1939. Adolf Hitler aroused the anger of the Western world as he systematically tried to destroy the Jewish people and all those he perceived as misfits, including homosexuals. After graduation from high school in 1941, I chose to attend Washington and Jefferson College; I had been there only three months when the Japanese bombed Pearl Harbor. Stretched out on the living room floor of Phi Delta Theta fraternity house in Washington, Pennsylvania, I listened, along with other members and pledges of the fraternity, to the radio broadcast describing the events that led to our entry into World War II. I had a sinking feeling in the pit of my stomach as I listened to President Roosevelt's speech. The only other time I could remember feeling that way was when, at the age of eight, I listened to the radio announcement of the invasion of Manchuria by the Japanese. In both cases, it was clear that human beings were murdering one another over the question of turf. The next several days at college were filled with uncertainty and anxiety: Many questioned whether they should even finish out the school year. When Christmas break came, we all went home for more discussion and some decision making.

The bombing of Pearl Harbor sent millions of people in the United States to places they had never heard of, to fight a war against genocide and raw aggression, both of which were symbols of a desire for world power and world control. Millions of lives in other parts of the world had been disrupted or destroyed and sacrificed on the altars of power and prejudice. Staying in school long enough to graduate was not possible. My family and I had long discussions at the supper table over whether I was really a conscientious objector or not. After deciding I could not be a conscientious objector and that I had to fight in this war, I had one choice to make: whether to wait to be drafted or to enlist.

Enlistment might let me finish out the school year, so I enlisted and was sent off for basic training to Fort Bragg, North Carolina. Having never been away from home, I was scared stiff. At age eighteen, I was taught how to protect myself in combat and how to kill. To prepare for battle and for combat training, we were sent to Camp Howze, Texas, where I became a part of the Headquarters Company in a field artillery battalion. From Texas, the field artillery outfit I was with shipped out to Europe. We went first to New York City, where thousands of us were then packed into an Italian luxury liner for a trip to Marseilles, France. We slept in bunks, piled five high, in what had been the ballroom, and we worried, even though we traveled in convoy, about German U-boats sending us all to the bottom of the Atlantic. After about a week, we passed through the Strait of Gibraltar on a sunny October afternoon. Africa was beautiful in the bright afternoon sun. We landed in Marseilles, France, at 5:00 p.m. With full packs, we marched uphill until 2:00 a.m. to a plateau fourteen miles north of Marseilles; we joined combat forces a few days later. We were on our way to the Colmar Gap.

During those months in cómbat in Europe, I settled in my own mind what I would like to do with my life. Perhaps because one sees the best and the worst of human nature in the armed forces, transformations occur regularly. Some of the worst people surprise you with their greatness; some of the best surprise you with their descent into the depths of depravity and meanness. One of the men in my section, very much in love with his girl back home, visited a brothel in a French city and bragged about it when he got back to our section. When I asked him if he would tolerate the same behavior from his girl back home, he said "God damn you, Righter, you ruined my evening!" But we remained friends. A superb Episcopal chaplain named Albert J. Dubois and my parish rector, Louis Hirshson, helped me in gentle ways to come to the decision to study for the priesthood in the Episcopal Church. They suggested I observe people while I was in the army, and begin to understand their idiosyncrasies and their behavior. Unlike St. Paul, I was not stricken blind on the road to Damascus. My call to the priesthood came through a gradual dawning of what I perceived God wanted me to do and be. I was finally able to say I felt called to the service of God through Jesus Christ in Holy Orders.

While that identification process was going on, the outfit that I was in fought its way through Europe. We slept in tents pitched in spots that were often half-covered with icy water. We went days without baths or shaves. We traveled on open trucks in ten-degree weather. We ate C rations, if we could light fires and heat them, and K rations if we could not. Just before Christmas, we were sent to the underbelly of the area where the Battle of the Bulge was being fought. On Christmas Eve, the chaplain celebrated Holy Communion in a French barn as we all knelt on the concrete floor amid the smells of farm animals. That night, in the joy and solemnity of the season, stripped of all the seasonal decorations we were used to, in the midst of the animals of God's creation, surrounded by a war of our own making, I knew this was the work God would have me do—help people to see God in the midst of life, and to help people find peace instead of war. By New Year's Eve, we were off into Germany and Austria.

On May 7, 1945, World War II in Europe ended, and I celebrated by getting hopelessly soused! One of the enlisted men in our section found two dozen bottles of champagne somewhere. One dozen went to the officers; seven of us enlisted men kept the rest. Since we were living in a five-story building in Innsbruck, Austria, we took our champagne and our canteen cups to the fifth floor for a party. Canteen cups hold a pint. By midnight, we had consumed all the champagne. It went right to my head and stayed there. In order to negotiate the stairs, I went down backward, on my hands and knees, from the fifth floor to the first.

World War II in Asia ended three months later. I heard the news while walking through the city of Reims, France, close to the famous cathedral. I entered that cathedral, kneeling in the first pew I could reach, and said prayers of thanksgiving for the end of hostilities. Although I gave thanks, I really did not understand the implications of the atomic bomb and what it had done in Japan. All I knew was that I could go home and restart my civilian life.

Although I studied for the priesthood at Berkeley Divinity School and was ordained, postwar changes occurred so rapidly and continuously that I rarely questioned the role, or depth, of the church during these years. The noise of progress and the incessant demand for programs and space drowned out specific questions and persistent questioners.

Certainly equality of the sexes emerged as a major issue following the war. Most women discovered their ability to work outside the home during the war, as industries begged them to join the labor force. After the war ended, many women continued to work, got college degrees, and entered professions. Although I could sense the magnitude of this change, it was not until a week's visit to the College of Preachers at the National Cathedral in Washington that I began to examine its implications. It was a quiet, meditative time, filled with opportunities for prayer and thoughtful consideration of my priestly and pastoral ministry. In the spring of 1965, I became a Fellow of the College and spent eight weeks studying and thinking. Washington, D.C., is a rich mix of what is beautiful and powerful about our political experiment. I studied at the

Library of Congress, walked among the cherry blossoms and spring azaleas, and absorbed the political debates; that intense period of time informed everything I did thereafter.

It became clear to me, for example, that equality of the sexes had to be addressed by the church. Not only was this feeling reinforced by the civil rights movement; it was also central to many debates about human dignity raised by objectors to the Vietnam War. Without thinking about it too consciously, I was undeniably moving from a middle-of-the-road, conservative position to that of a liberal in both politics and religion.

Shortly after my consecration as Bishop of Iowa in 1972, three of the clergy at my second Diocesan Convention moved that we have a straw vote on whether women could be ordained. They moved that we vote by orders, meaning clergy and laity would vote as distinctly different groups and the measure had to pass in both. Under our procedural rules, I called for a clergy roll call. When it was over, 50 percent said yes and 50 percent said no. My chancellor, Ross Sidney, said I could break the tie. He was a recognized defense lawyer, and a pragmatist about canon law, and I respected his wisdom greatly. People began coming to the platform where I sat, telling me how and why I ought to vote a certain way, while some of the clergy stood at the back of the room and glared angrily at me. The tension in the room was electric. A priest from New Zealand went out of his way to tell me that the bishops in New Zealand, when asked to break a tie, always voted to preserve the status quo. I let my stomach calm down a bit and voted for ordination of women to the priesthood. The laity clapped and cheered. In Iowa, they were usually more progressive than the clergy, and they voted overwhelmingly in favor of ordination of women. Fifteen percent of the clergy left the diocese after that vote, moving to other dioceses, where they believed the ordination of women would not carry. But theirs was a pipe dream. By 1976, the entire Episcopal church had approved the ordination of women to the priesthood. At the time of my retirement in 1989, 33 percent of the clergy in full-time positions in Iowa were women.

After that convention, a few of the clergy urged me to tell everyone where I stood, as their bishop, on the issue of homosexuality. This insistence came almost immediately after the straw vote on the ordination of women. And there it was: the clear link between homophobia and misogyny. Because we were beginning to have serious conversations about homosexuality, I agreed to write a statement. My first impulse was simply to state that homosexuals were also the children of God, but it seemed best to consult some authorities before writing my statement. The American Psychiatric Association, among others, said that homosexuality could be "treated." So my statement to the people of Iowa reminded them that the church was not a therapeutic organization, but a redemptive one, and I said I thought we should keep up our redemptive work and let psychiatric counselors do the therapeutic work. Within a day, I knew my error. A priest called to tell me what a fine statement I had made, and when that particular priest praised my work, I knew I had made a mistake.

From that time on, I became more aware of and more sensitive to homosexual people and their inclusion in the church. Surely the church needed to take the lead in embracing all the children of God. The American Psychiatric Association reversed its position in 1973 and said that homosexuality was not an "illness." The American Psychological Association took a similar stand in 1975. In Iowa, academic communities, such as the University of Iowa, Iowa State University, and the University of Northern Iowa, led the way in discussing homosexual rights, and many younger people in those communities "came out," at least to their clergy. The Rev. Robert Holzhammer, rector of Trinity Church in Iowa City, and his assistant, the Rev. Anne Baker, were helpful to me in subtle ways they might not have recognized; they deepened my understanding of what was happening. My neighbor in Nebraska, the Rt. Rev. Robert Varley, the Episcopal bishop there, became part of a national committee to meet with and listen to gay and lesbian people. Occasionally, I heard him describe these meetings. As I heard it, the beginning was only a groping for ideas. Little came from these efforts, but the process of gradual and steady change began. We were still in a time, I think, when bishops were not trusted with information about one's personal life. Hints were dropped in a subtle manner as "tests." Would a bishop tell people that someone was homosexual? Would he use that against someone? There were some bishops who were known to be homophobes, some who were trying to understand, and a few who were understanding but quiet about it. Unconfirmed gossip had it that at least five bishops were gay. Integrity (a national organization for gay and lesbian people in the Episcopal church) was started by Louie Crew in 1974. While sympathetic to Louie's effort, I watched from a distance.

In the early 1980s, the Diocese of Iowa began a companion relationship with the Diocese of Brechin in Scotland, and my horizon broadened greatly. That relationship got me in touch in a fresh way with the greater Anglican Communion throughout the world. In Scotland, I met people from India and Africa—committed Christians, participants in the institution we call the church, professional people, blue-collar workers, management people—who represented "all sorts and conditions of men." Their homes were not unlike ours—but colder. While I was there, usually in August, we went to bed with hot-water bottles to warm up the sheets. Peat or coal fires burned in the fireplace almost all day. Tim Eng, an American priest working in Melrose, Scotland (home of Sir Walter Scott), lives in a fourteen-room rectory. It's a beautiful house of stone construction and has central heat. His first month there, he kept the whole house at sixty-eight degrees and did not use the fireplaces. His heating bill that month was almost five hundred pounds, or somewhere in the neighborhood of eight hundred dollars for one month's warmth.

Although the climate was cold, the people were welcoming and warmhearted. Such a climate occasionally produces stubborn and dour people as well as warm and welcoming ones. I also met those who lived in what were called "areas of multiple deprivation." At that time, 25 percent of the population of Scotland lived in what was government housing for the poor. In comparison with such housing in the United States, these areas were neater and cleaner; they had grass and bushes around them and were well kept. A look beneath the surface showed other differences, however. In winter, the interior walls in the apartments would be covered with ice. The central heat was not sufficient for the buildings, and there were no fireplaces. One mother of four, pregnant with her fifth child, told me the father of this child was her social worker. Sometimes two and three generations of the same family, primarily mothers with small children, lived there and had no regular work, no live-in father, and very little hope for a change.

Gradually, I found myself understanding in a new and concrete way what it is to be marginalized and alienated. The process of becoming a liberal, begun some years before, was becoming complete. I was also undergoing some kind of personal conversion. It started on a New Hampshire ski slope.

That day, while my son, Richard, skied, I spent a lot of time thinking. It was in the late 1960s, and I was feeling depressed about my job, and about the church and her future. I watched the skiers, many of whom were my good friends, and saw excitement and joy on their faces. In late afternoon, as the sun began to go down, my son and I left for home. He was exhausted but happy. I was exhilarated. A conversion process had begun within me. I had affirmed, within myself, that I believed in a loving, compassionate God who cared deeply about me. The feeling I had was akin to the one I had about becoming a priest. It was like flying in an airplane through darkness, looking out the window, and then seeing a lightning flash illuminate the landscape brightly for a few seconds. I was clear about the fact that I would do whatever I could, for the rest of my life, to share my faith and make it understandable to the world around me. I would try to enlist the help of others in declaring God's love.

As a by-product, I found myself much more ready to become involved in correcting injustice—even ready to fight for correcting it! After one of my trips to Scotland, working at our companion relationship, I came home and called *The Witness*, an Episcopal church publication dedicated to promoting peace and justice, and subscribed for all of our Iowa clergy. I asked the diocese to join me in my efforts to raise funds for the needs of people in various places throughout the world— in Swaziland, Scotland, Guatemala, the Philippines, and in the cities of the United States.

Injustice was also close to home: Iowa and particularly the farmers of Iowa were going through what industrial giants were later to label "downsizing." To farmers, this meant larger and larger farms were dominating agribusiness, and small farmers were in trouble. People in Iowa called it "the farm crisis." This crisis had historical roots but had become more accelerated and more noticeable in the 1980s, erupting into a full-fledged crisis. Banks foreclosed, stock and equipment were sold, and families were broken. Some injustices are not readily set right.

As the eighties came to a close, it was time to retire. Some of the resulting changes were radical: I sought and received a divorce; I remarried; I looked for a support community that was not identical to my work community. The trauma of major change was eased considerably by Frank Griswold, the Bishop of Chicago, who asked me to be the interim rector at Immanuel Church in Rockford, Illinois. The people in that parish were a welcoming community and I rediscovered myself as a parish priest.

The Immanuel parish is a unique institution, forged under the leadership of the person who was there before I became interim rector, the Rev. J. Cardone, and by the skills and convictions of a variety of laypeople. For several years, the Episcopal Church had been promoting the idea of giving 50 percent of its income away. Parishes and dioceses were both asked to make that a long-range goal. Iowa had been a leader in this endeavor before I ever became bishop. Support for the idea in the diocese had helped us greatly in achieving financial stability, as men and women worked hard at sharing their substance with others. When I got to Rockford, I discovered the idea had become a reality in that parish. Several different outreach programs for the chronically mentally ill, for the socially disadvantaged, for the physically disabled, and for the homeless were combined in an overarching unit that used one of the parish's buildings every day of the week and every weekend. The programs were operated by a staff of several people who were guided and managed by a lapsed Roman Catholic layperson who adopted the principles of the Mennonite community. To be rector, interim or permanent, I discovered, meant being president of the board of trustees leading that superb effort. While I had always had a staff of some kind during my ministry, the management of those various groups of people had always focused on maintaining and expanding the life of a parish church. But here I discovered the complexity of not only managing a staff but one doing outreach work that was new to me. Called upon to put my skills where my creedal mouth was, I found that staff taught me a great deal about justice, love, and compassion for others in a crash program of a few months. Constant funding needed to be sought from a variety of places, not just from the people of the parish. The state of Illinois was a very willing provider of funds for most of the outreach programs because Immanuel was almost without competitors, virtually alone in providing these services in Rockford. The city of Rockford, a blue-collar community specializing in tool-making and allied industries, is the second-largest city in the state of Illinois, with 150,000 people, after Chicago, which has a population of about 3 million. Rockford is in north-central Illinois, farm country. Immanuel Church's efforts could be pointed to throughout the state as a real possibility for smaller communities. More than 50 percent of the money the parish had coming in was spent on those outside the parish.

Even in retirement, there are opportunities for learning that are unusual. Besides that, I found I had not only pastoral skills that could be useful to people in the parish but also conceptual knowledge that made it possible for people involved in the parish programs to extend themselves. It was a delightful and fascinating seven months.

As that assignment came to an end, I was invited by Jack Spong, the Bishop of Newark, to come to his diocese and assist him with his duties. He wanted me to help him shape the position of suffragan, or assistant, bishop. He needed help with the crises that occurred with some regularity in his 140 parishes. His cathedral congregation needed more supervision and care than he could give it. And the cities of his diocese—Newark, Paterson, Jersey City, and Clifton—and the parishes within them needed attention. I accepted his invitation and began work in Newark on Labor Day of 1989. It was stimulating and exciting. There were city parishes and suburban parishes. Some people were extremely wealthy; some were desperately poor. There were Chinese people, Korean people, African people, islanders from the Caribbean. After seventeen years in Iowa, where an interracial marriage was defined as a union between a Norwegian and a Swede, the many races from all over the globe in the Diocese of Newark were a revelation and stimulus to mission and ministry. They were symbolic of what was happening in the Anglican Communion throughout the world.

Jack asked me to be the Bishop for the cathedral church. It, like Rockford, was unique. For a variety of reasons, too complex to describe here, the cathedral people were out of synch with their bishop. On most Sundays, I helped Jack Spong with his visitations to parishes and missions in the diocese. But the first Easter I was there, it seemed wise for me to visit the cathedral parish to confirm candidates and to celebrate the Eucharist. Ninety-nine percent of the members of that cathedral are black. An occasional white face is seen in the congregation, and there is one white person who is a regular communicant. I decided on that Easter that I would call a spade a shovel and preach a sermon about the need to stop the hostility toward the bishop and start reconciliation efforts. Members of the vestry knew what I intended. While the senior warden reluctantly approved of my idea, the rest of the vestry had a secret meeting on Easter Eve to plan how to counteract whatever I might say in my sermon. On Easter Day, as soon as I had finished preaching, urging a change of attitude, the coroner of Essex County, also an undertaker and a member of the cathedral parish, stood up in the balcony and proclaimed quite loudly, "Bishop Righter, you have just insulted our intelligence!" We went on with our Easter service in a few minutes, but at a parish meeting immediately after the service, some members of the vestry tried, for their own reasons, to sabotage any reconciliation between the people and their bishop. One man came running down the aisle of the cathedral, shouting at me, waving his arms, and acting as if he might hit me. I remember thinking, I wish he would hit me. I can take care of myself, and it would get this meeting down to rock-bottom reality. But he stopped short of violence. The meeting ended with little resolved, but the boil of anger and hatred had been lanced, and its poison drained out over the next several years. Again, as in Rockford, the uniqueness of the situation meant I had to do a crash course in learning the basics of an urban/suburban diocese that had gone through shattering upheaval over a twenty-year period.

Jack Spong had also done a lot of hard work while inviting the people to participate in reshaping the social contract. Several years prior to my arrival, the whole diocese had done a study of human sexuality that was quite thorough and solid, one I remember reading while I was still in Iowa. At that time, I wrote Jack a note congratulating him and his people for the work they had done. The people, especially the clergy, had developed an understanding about sexuality that could roughly be described as "corporate," or diocesan. A special ministry for lesbian and gay people had been founded in the city of Hoboken, with All Saints Church as its base. The rector of All Saints, Geoff Curtiss, was young, aggressive, and innovative. The people of the parish were, by and large, employed at upper-middle-class jobs in New York City but chose to live across the river in New Jersey. Their city, once famous as the home of Frank Sinatra and of Maxwell House coffee, had been a blue-collar community and was becoming, as people say nowadays, "gentrified." With diocesan support, the parish became the center for a new ministry, named Oasis. A young deacon named Robert Williams, a graduate of Episcopal Divinity School, had been called to and had accepted the position of director for that ministry.

In the fall of 1989, the question of getting Robert ordained to the priesthood was something that consumed a lot of discussion. He was gay. Many gay people had been ordained in the Episcopal Church's history, but it had been done quietly and without an emphasis on their sexuality. If they had same-sex partners, that was kept quiet, as well. In view of the Diocese of Newark's special study, and the special ministry Robert had to the gay community in the diocese, Jack wanted this ordination to be done openly and honestly. So he called the Presiding Bishop to tell him that he was going to ordain Robert to the priesthood, and that Robert was gay and had a same-sex partner. The Presiding Bishop suggested that he write to the then Bishop of Dallas, Donis Patterson, since Robert had originally been from that diocese. Jack agreed to do that. Then he decided, again in the spirit of honesty and openness, that he should write to every bishop in the church to notify them of the ordination.

When the then Bishop of Fort Worth, Clarence Pope, got the letter, he called the press and set off a firestorm over the ordination. The static about that calmed down and the ordination was held, with three bishops present—the Bishop of Newark, the retired Bishop of Maine, Fred Wolf, who was the preacher, and myself. One person stood up and objected to the ordination. The content of his objection had been dealt with over and over again in the Diocese of Newark by responsible persons and committees. The bishop, after listening carefully and saying clearly that the various committees and commissions of the diocese had heard the objection made and had dealt with it thoroughly, said the ordination would take place and announced he would continue. Robert Williams was ordained to the priesthood and the firestorm began again, with Bishop Spong at its center. Fred Wolf and I were ignored, as were all the bishops who had ordained gay or lesbian people in the recent past. Conservative anger needed a focal point and it found it in Jack Spong. For a brief moment in history, it garnered more support than it deserved.

Robert had become famous overnight. He had lots of invitations to speak throughout the United States about his experiences and his ministry, but, as a new seminary graduate, he was not ready for such public exposure. Seminary prepares you for the excitement of the priesthood, and it gives you a sense of the history of the ministry; it does not prepare you to be a pioneer. Because of the unique place and the pioneering spirit of Oasis in the life of the Episcopal Church, Robert became an instant pioneer. He was expected to make statements and answer questions that even the most seasoned of clergy would have had trouble fielding. According to his autobiography, *Just As I Am*, during one of those speaking engagements—in Detroit, Michigan—a priest in the audience asked him a series of pointed questions, including one about the tradition of celibacy in the church. Unhappy with Robert's negative comments on that tradition, the priest asked, "Do you really think Mother Teresa's life would be significantly enhanced—," and Robert cut him off with, "If she got laid? Yes! I am saying that everyone's life is significantly enhanced by sexual activity, and significantly diminished by the lack of it." The firestorm broke out again, and again Jack Spong was at the center of things. The controversy erupted in the midst of the annual Diocesan Convention, where Jack was the presiding officer. Unable to leave his post for any protracted time, he asked me to meet with the board of directors of Oasis when they met with Robert. I found them depressed and confused. Their pioneering dream for a ministry to gay and lesbian persons was suddenly in grave danger. Some of the members of the board were also in grave danger. Many of them were "in the closet" as gay or lesbian people. For some, their jobs might be in jeopardy if their employers found out they were gay or lesbian. The person the board had chosen to lead them in that ministry had, intentionally or not, failed them.

Robert really did not understand the full commitments of ordination in the Episcopal Church. To be ordained, one must have an invitation from a group of people to serve in their midst. Although Robert had accepted the invitation to come and work, he had accepted engagements from all over the United States, as well. Instead of staying home and putting Oasis on track, this inexperienced young priest got beyond himself. The subtleties of dealing with the media and their questions were beyond his experience. Ordained in December, he faced all of this in February. In that brief a time, Robert had managed to fail thoroughly.

The board, in dealing with that failure, had to deal with their own failure, as well. We spent a great deal of time in the meeting so that each person could speak his or her own painful thoughts. The consensus seemed to be that Robert should resign. I suggested that all of us, especially Robert, would need some time to absorb the meaning of what was happening. The meeting adjourned to give him that time. This also gave the directors time to absorb their own sense of failure, their own danger at being "outed," if that occurred, and to give serious thought to the next step for them as a board and for Oasis.

In the next twenty-four hours, Robert Williams resigned from the ministry of Oasis. It is my understanding, from what others have said, that the Rev. Carter Hayward, theologian at Episcopal Divinity School in Cambridge, Massachusetts, and one of Robert Williams's teachers during his time in seminary, persuaded him to resign during an early morning telephone conversation.

In those few days, I became acquainted in a new and fresh way with people who were openly lesbian or gay. I had never in my life worked as closely or in the midst of such a crisis with that many lesbian and gay people. I saw faithful, committed church people. I saw people who had been in same-sex partnerships for years, often celebrating twenty-five years of life together. I saw people hungry for the church to become a "safe" place for them. I saw people hopeful that Jack Spong and the Diocese of Newark would provide a haven that would provide a model the rest of the church could follow. I saw people very uncertain about the church, and very careful about who knew about their sexual orientation. The clergy were particularly cautious.

I began to feel in more urgent and profound ways the dilemma of homosexual people in the church. Here were people who had been faithful to the church's purpose all of their lives. Here were people faithful to their partners for years. Here were people who looked to the church to provide moral leadership, to open the doors to health, wholeness, and healing. And yet the church was resisting, just as she and some of her leaders resisted equality for women, equal opportunity for the poor, and civil rights. I began to see the links among homophobia, misogyny, racism, and classism—all efforts to reduce the inherent worth of another human being. My long pilgrimage—seventy-four years and still in progress—is a gradual one. But it has also been accompanied by great moments of discovery. The Diocese of Newark, with its risks, magnificent friendships, and urgent needs, revealed the pressing necessity for decisions now.

CHAPTER 2

"Are We Gonna Ordain 'Em or Not?"

THE YEAR WAS 1972, the occasion my first House of Bishops meeting, in New Orleans, Louisiana. The questioner was Jim Duncan, Bishop of Southeast Florida. His question, which addressed whether or not the House of Bishops would ordain gay men, followed a straw vote over the ordination of women. Clearly, even in 1972, this was a vexing issue. Many bishops had already ordained some gay men. The very thought of such ordinations raised the ire of others.

The House of Bishops was, for me, a community of heroes. I had been confirmed (made a full member) in the Episcopal Church in 1937. In ways that teenagers don't completely understand, it was a major event in my life. A new suit, a brand-new leather-bound prayer book, its very thin pages making it almost too special to use, the whole family getting to church (including my aunt, who was in a wheelchair)—all symbolized that something special was happening. A mysterious person called a bishop was coming for the service. He was in his eighties and did not have a car; he traveled by trolley. He was known for saying his prayers as he rode on the trolley car, because he was too tired to pray when he got home at night. He carried his own suitcase. To get to our church, the bishop had to walk up a steep hill for about a half a mile, carrying that suitcase. All of that added to the mystique about this man. Francis M. Taitt, the Bishop of Pennsylvania, did not behave like an aristocrat or a prince of the church at all. As the service began and he preached the sermon, he spoke simply and directly, with the proper amount of ritual and decorum. The church seated 750 people. Regular attendance was fifty. In the midst of the service, the furnace quit, and the building got cold. To outsiders looking in, the scene might have suggested an almost-empty church struggling for existence. To me, that day was memorable because it included my first real experience with a bishop—a plainspoken, kindly, ancient person who had no trappings of office and did not insist on any, yet who fulfilled his duties with simple dignity.

My second real encounter with a bishop occurred on the day I went to see the Bishop of Pittsburgh about entering Holy Orders. I was still in the uniform of an enlisted field artillery sergeant and World War II had ended. I had come home for a two-week leave on my way from Europe to a center in Texas where I was to be discharged. Hostilities in Europe and Japan had not only ended; there was a resurgence of interest in great humanitarian ideals, in a world community at peace.

I found a vibrant, vigorous person in Austin Pardue. It took him ten minutes to ask me all the questions he wanted to and to dispense the advice he would give to all of us who were in seminary in the years immediately following World War II. "Work in a coal mine or steel mill; your ordination depends on it."

He did not have any authority to do that, but we believed him and, by our belief, gave him the authority he needed. I found a job in the Homestead plant of U.S. Steel

and went to work in the metallurgical section. It took me into
the mill for part of the day and into the laboratory for the
other part. Bishop Pardue gave us all careful instructions.
"Don't get preachy. Don't try to convert everybody. Get to
know what it's like to work in a mill. If people ask you questions about your future, give them truthful answers. But don't
volunteer a lot of stuff about 'churchy' things." I worked in
that mill for several months and obeyed the bishop's instructions. I made one good friend. He was helpful to me in learning about the safety rules in the mill. We rode the streetcar to
work every day and talked about the weather, the Pittsburgh
Pirates, politics, the steel mill and its bosses, and a lot of other
things. He knew all the four-letter words and could use them
both imaginatively and appropriately. The day came for me to
leave the mill and go off to seminary. I told my boss I was leaving. Word got around. My friend with the colorful vocabulary
came up to me and declared, "You're leaving!" Remembering
the bishop's instruction about trying not to smear religion on
everyone, I simply said, "You're right. I am." With a great
deal of unexpressed impatience, my friend said, "What are
you going to do?" Again following the bishop's instructions,
and therefore not volunteering much (although telling the
truth), I said, "I'm going back to school." My friend's impatience got the best of him. He put his hands on his hips and
said, "Damn it, I know you're going back to school. That
word has gotten around the mill. But what in hell are you
going to do when you get there? You gonna study accounting
and come back here and take all the money out of this mill?
You gonna study metallurgy and come back here and help us
make better steel? What in hell you gonna do?" A moment of
truth had come. The bishop had said, "Tell the truth!" So I
did. I said to my friend, "I'm going to seminary to learn how
to be a priest in the Episcopal Church!" My friend kept his
hands on his hips and said, loud and clear, "Well, for Christ's

sake!" Then his eyes twinkled and he got a funny grin on his face. "That's what it's all about, isn't it?" I shall never forget that exchange. The bishop's idea of having his students for Holy Orders work in a steel mill or a coal mine produced not only a set of singular experiences but an unforgettable frame in which to review them.

It was an unusual but helpful launch into seminary, into ordination, into the ordained ministry in the Episcopal Church, and, eventually, into the episcopate in Iowa. The day after I was elected bishop in October 1971, Bishop Pardue called me on the phone to congratulate me. He began the conversation by saying, "Since I'm the one who got you in all this trouble by ordaining you in the first place, I called to congratulate you and to wish you well." He was retired, although still very interested in what was happening in the lives of those he knew and cared about.

Prior to going to seminary, I still had to finish up a university degree. I decided to do that at the University of Pittsburgh. Knowing that, Bishop Pardue sent me to the community of Rector, Pennsylvania, an hour east of Pittsburgh, to start a church "from scratch." His instructions to me went like this: "The present Bishop of Arizona tried to start a church there when he was rector of Calvary Church, Pittsburgh, and he failed. The present Bishop of Western New York tried to start a church there when he was rector of Calvary Church and he failed. If you fail, it's no skin off your nose, so go try." It worked. I didn't fail. In 1989, I attended the fortieth anniversary of that church and saw many of my former Sunday school students filling responsible roles as leaders in what has become St. Michael's in the Valley, one of the strong parishes in the Diocese of Pittsburgh.

Bishop Taitt and Bishop Pardue are examples of what I expected to find in the House of Bishops—visionary people, vigorous people, people not impressed with the trappings of the office but capable of filling the office quietly and to the credit of God's people. When I was in seminary, that's the kind of mystique that surrounded the office. These were people who had the wisdom necessary to make appropriate decisions about the future direction of the church, and the courage to lead people in that direction. Our Presiding Bishop at that time, Henry K. Sherrill, was a founder of the National Council of Churches and there were other such visionaries. The Bishop of Washington, whose name was Angus Dun, was known in his diocese as "Black Angus" because of his work on behalf of civil rights. The Bishop of New Hampshire, Tod Hall, was known as a fanatic about democracy because of the way in which he protected people's right to speak out on controversial issues. The Presiding Bishop, who consecrated me in 1972, John Hines, had led the Episcopal Church into a program for empowering the poor that was copied by almost all of the mainline denominations in the years afterward. Bishop Hines developed his understanding of the need for that program by walking the streets of cities, especially New York, sometimes at great risk to himself, and talking with people he met. These bishops were unusual, and for hundreds—even thousands—of people, they were, and still are, heroes.

It was, therefore, not just a surprise but a shock to find tensions and the heated arguments with regard to a number of issues when I joined the House of Bishops in 1972. In open session, we had discussed proposed revisions to the Book of Common Prayer and had taken a straw vote on the ordination of women. In that straw vote, the issue passed. Not until four years later did the General Convention say women could be ordained. I now realize that it was no accident at all that the Episcopal Church voted to ordain women in 1976 and had its first formal discussion about the ordination of homosexuals in the very next convention, in 1979.

Some bishops have told me that the only use they made of the psychiatric examinations required of all Candidates for Holy Orders was to determine if someone was homosexual, so they could refuse to ordain the person. I am still saddened by that. The necessity for a psychiatric exam arose in the House of Bishops when it was proposed that all bishops be given a psychiatric exam before their consecration to determine if they had serious problems of some kind that would hamper their functioning as a bishop. After discussion, it was decided that all Candidates for Holy Orders would be required to undergo a psychiatric exam before being approved for ordination. Using a psychiatric test has many appropriate applications; searching for homosexuals is not among them. The label *homosexual* seemed to trigger deeper fears—the image of predatory males who tried to seduce male children and teenagers. In that charged atmosphere, we began our discussion. In order to do so, we went into executive session—doors closed, no one allowed in except bishops.

Iowans were surprised when I told them about the discussion on homosexuality. They were, like the bishops, of many different opinions on the subject. They had never seriously discussed the subject. While it may have occurred to them that there were some homosexual clergy, they tended to think ordinations were the bishop's responsibility. Many Iowans had had clergy who were gay and who had been magnificent pastors for them.

Without understanding it very well, both the House of Bishops and the whole of the Episcopal Church began a serious pilgrimage into the question of human sexuality. Every House of Bishops meeting since 1972 has had on its agenda some aspect of human sexuality. Between meetings of the General Convention, the House of Bishops has interim meetings—at least one a year, in the fall, and ever since our General Convention in Phoenix, Arizona, in 1991, two meetings a year. At one of those interim meetings in the early 1970s, held in Mexico, we had one of our straw votes on the ordination of women. The majority vote in favor of the issue had increased, and with it, the intensity of the emotional debate. After the straw vote made it obvious that the number in favor had increased, we took a break and went outside into the cool air. The then Bishop of Milwaukee, Charles Gaskell, enraged by the vote, obsessed by the issue, charged at me during the break, hit me hard on the chest with his fist, and said, "If that passes at the General Convention in 1976, it will be your fault!" I can still feel the physical impact of that blow. At the General Convention of 1976, through an addition to the canons (church law), we voted to permit women to be ordained to the priesthood and the episcopate, having previously voted (1970) to permit women to be ordained to the diaconate. Some raged. Some bishops tried to threaten the whole Episcopal Church with claims that they would now have to leave if women were to be ordained. No bishops did. Some priests and some laity did leave. Their numbers were less than 1 percent of our membership.

Robert Cromey, rector of Trinity Church in San Francisco, in a paper he titles "The Fall of the House of Bishops," argues that bishops have abdicated their role as leaders. In the past, Cromey states, the bishops led the church in liturgy, social service, and social action. Now, he suggests, they are staunchly quiet, middle-of-the-road, and harmless. I would say, based on my experience, they are staunchly quiet and middle-of-the-road, but far from harmless. The vituperative name-calling has increased in amount and intensity, much as the violence in our country has increased. During the General Convention in Phoenix, Arizona, in 1991, when the retired Bishop of Oklahoma tried, through a motion in the House of Bishops, to have me and the Bishop of Washington, D.C., censured for, as he said, "breaking the collegiality of the

House of Bishops" (we had both ordained a homosexual person with a same-sex partner), the extent of our collegiality was clear. *Collegiality* was, and still is, a code word for *uniformity*. That is an impossible goal in a group as complex as the House of Bishops in the Episcopal Church, and hardly a desirable one. As a result of this discussion, the Presiding Bishop was asked to convene an extra meeting of the House of Bishops each year in an attempt to develop better relationships among the members of the House. The motion, which was substituted for the motion of censure, canceled it. The discussion was held in executive session. The next day, a member of Episcopalians United (a conservative caucus) said to the Bishop of Newark, "I'm so glad you said what you said in the executive session yesterday!" It seems that the House of Bishops had been bugged. No one, on that day, seemed to know who had placed the electronic device in the meeting room. Yet there was no doubt it had been done, because people knew not only what we had talked about but the words that had been used and who spoke them. The Bishop of Pittsburgh, a strong supporter of Episcopalians United, denied that they had done the bugging. Whether anyone knows to this day who it was who placed the bug doesn't matter. The action serves as a symbol of the kind of spirit loose in the church these days—surreptitious, sneaky listening in on a closed meeting!

It is my personal opinion that that same spirit was behind the presentment of me. The composition of the presenters, six of whom were new to the House of Bishops after the convention in Phoenix, Arizona, needs to be looked at carefully. Seven of them are from the South or the Southwest. Two are from the north-central part of the United States. One is from the West. Four have consistently refused to accept and/or obey the canon that reads "No one shall be denied access to the selection process for ordination in this church because of race, color, ethnic origin, sex, national origin, marital status, sexual orientation [added in 1994], disabilities or age" (Title III, Canon 4, Sec. 1). All of those four were elected and consecrated as bishops at least four years after we had adopted the canon permitting the ordination of women. Their opposition to this canon is accommodated through a statement called "the conscience clause," which permits particular bishops, for the sake of their own consciences, to abstain from ordaining women. We have always been a communion with particular sensitivity to another's conscience, so the conscience clause was one we tolerated. What we couldn't tolerate, what in fact was a total surprise to most of us, was the way in which the conscience clause became a mechanism for establishing diocesan policy. Bishops whose consciences would not permit them to ordain a woman refused to allow a woman access, and refused even to consider ways in which the dioceses they were leading could consider the subject. Some women, in some dioceses, were ridiculed for even trying to discuss the subject. The canons had been amended to permit ordination of women. But by employing the conscience clause, bishops could bar the ordination of women, even though such behavior constituted a violation of the canons of the Episcopal Church. Four of the presenters were in just such a position as they pointed their accusatory fingers at me.

STEPHEN BAYNE'S LIFE and work as a priest and bishop embraced more variety, depth, and achievement than that of almost any other bishop in the United States or in the Anglican Communion. He was chaplain to Episcopal students at Columbia University, rector of the parish of St. John's in Northampton, Massachusetts, Bishop of the Diocese of Olympia in the state of Washington, and first executive officer of the Anglican Communion. Stephen was largely responsible for helping the whole Anglican Communion build a sense of international identity it had not had. As assistant to the Presiding Bishop, when John Hines was the PB, and acting dean of General Theological Seminary, he contributed greatly to that sense of community in the United States.

Although his achievements were expansive, throughout his entire ministry he kept a personal and pastoral touch. When he became rector of a parish in Northampton, Massachusetts, he heard the people complain about the short time their clergy stayed in their parish. One evening, during a vestry meeting, he told the vestry he had planted a cherry tree in the backyard of the rectory. When his senior warden asked why, he replied, "Because I like cherry pie!" The senior warden, a realist and one of the chief complainers about clergy who stayed only a short time, responded by saying, "It's going to take several years for you to get enough cherries off that tree to make a pie!" The rector replied, "I know. I can wait!" The planting of the cherry tree became a significant pastoral act. In a few days, everyone was talking about this new rector who was going to stay long enough to get enough cherries for a pie! As it turned out Stephen Bayne did not stay long enough to see his tree come to fruition. But he cared enough about the people of St. John's Church to notice their anxiety and speak to it in symbolic terms.

In the latter years of his ministry, he worked with the Presiding Bishop, John Hines, on some special concerns. A group of bishops during those years, led by Henry Louttit, presented James Pike, the Bishop of California, to be tried for heresy. Bishop Hines asked Stephen Bayne to chair a group of bishops to consider the whole idea of heresy in the twentieth century. The committee report, known as the Bayne Report and presented to the General Convention in 1967, was a thorough and thoughtful piece of work. It recommended, among other things, that it take a vote of two-thirds of the House of Bishops before a heresy trial of a bishop could go forward. It also recommended the idea of disassociation be used if someone in the House of Bishops took some action that the rest of the house did not like. The committee, an Advisory Committee on Theological Freedom and Social Responsibilities, was to provide a framework for collegial behavior on the part of the House of Bishops. The committee's description of the idea of disassociation is as follows:

"Without censuring or condemning any individual for his ideas, the Church may find it necessary, on occasion, to disassociate itself publicly from theological views which it considers to be seriously subversive of essential Christian truths."

All of that language sounds nicely irenic. It is designed to put some distance between the bishop who has disturbed the waters and the rest of the members of the House. In the phrase "without censuring or condemning any individual for his ideas," one can see the spirit intended. In recent usage, it has turned out to be anything but conciliatory. Our historical memory as a people is short. The passionate anger capable of being aroused by issues surrounding human sexuality, coupled with the absence of historical memory, can convert the purpose of the Bayne Report into a witch-hunt, as was apparent when some attempted to censure Jack Spong. The nicely phrased title composed by the committee that produced the Bayne Report—an Advisory Committee on Theological Freedom and Social Responsibility—proved a goal impossible to realize.

The resolution of disassociation directed at Jack Spong came into being around the fallout that resulted from the Robert Williams ordination. But another ordination rose on the theological horizon. Barry Stopfel, a graduate of Union Theological Seminary, a part-time lay assistant to the

Rev. Jack Croneberger, rector of the Church of the Atonement in Tenafly, New Jersey, and part-time employee of the Diocese of Newark in the area of Christian Education Resources, was qualified in all ways and ready for ordination. Four other people from the Diocese of Newark were also ready and just as qualified. Jack Spong, in his usual thorough and thoughtful way, called the Presiding Bishop to tell him that he was about to ordain another homosexual male living in a monogamous same-sex relationship and that his name was Barry Stopfel. The Presiding Bishop asked that Barry's ordination be postponed until after the meeting of the House of Bishops in September 1990. The purpose of the postponement was to give the House a chance to deliberate on the issue of human sexuality without more serious provocation than that which already existed. The resolution of disassociation had come out of the Presiding Bishop's Council of Advice (composed of the vice presidents or presidents of each one of the provinces of the Episcopal Church) re: the Williams ordination. It should be noted that the Presiding Bishop's Council of Advice, in shaping the resolution of disassociation, refused to allow Jack to meet with them. Although the Bayne Report advised such access, when Jack Spong asked for a chance to meet with the council, he was told by the Presiding Bishop that the bishops needed to ventilate their feelings without his being present. Later a participant told Jack that in the discussions it was determined that he was too powerful for them. At the meeting of the House of Bishops in 1990, the bishops of the Episcopal Church voted, after long and heated debate, to disassociate themselves from Bishop Spong's action and the action of the Diocese of Newark in ordaining Robert Williams. It was clear in the heat of the moment that people wanted vengeance. The purpose and spirit of the Bayne Report had been perverted.

In a sermon that Jack Spong preached at St. George's

Church, Maplewood, New Jersey, some years later, he said this about the vote taken at the House of Bishops in September 1990:

> My opponents, who believed the vote would be overwhelmingly in their favor, were stunned to record a narrow 80–76 majority, with two abstentions, one of which was mine. The other abstention was a retired bishop who was completely supportive of me but felt that retired bishops should not vote. If the two abstaining bishops had voted their convictions, then one changed vote could have caused the defeat of that motion for lack of a majority. Following that vote, the Presiding Bishop allowed me the privilege of addressing the House. I did so for forty-five minutes. When that speech was over, two things of great import occurred. First, at least a dozen bishops indicated to me that if they could have heard that speech before they voted, they would have changed their vote. Secondly, two bishops came out of the closet to me privately that evening. Both were married. One had voted for me, one against me. The one who voted against me had tears in his eyes and said he could never be soft on this issue. Being publicly opposed to gay issues was, he felt, his only defense against exposure.

After my retirement, when I joined the Diocese of Newark as assisting bishop, I gradually met the various staff people and got to know them. Barry Stopfel, a very thoughtful and creative person, was among them. We were both natives of Pennsylvania. We were both deeply interested in developing new ideas in Christian education. Barry helped orient me about the Diocese of Newark and the city itself. We found a lot to talk about whenever he passed my office door. During one of our conversations, I discovered Barry had been to Union Seminary in preparation for ordination in the Episcopal Church. He was a Candidate for Holy Orders in the Diocese of Newark. By background, by education, and by the screening process every diocese in the Episcopal Church has, he was one of the best-qualified persons for Holy Orders I had ever met. Throughout his screening and his education, he and his partner, Will, had been quite open about their relationship. They did not flaunt their sexual orientation, but they did not hide it, either.

I hope now that the context and the setting for the presentment of me with charges of heresy can be seen clearly. The Episcopal Church had become a heated microcosm of the battle over the changing roles of men and women, over the need to understand sexuality more clearly, over the clash between the past and the future. Many significant institutions in our society, and in the societies of other parts of our world, were wrestling with similar questions. Practically every major Christian denomination in the United States and some parts of Judaism had already made decisions about ordaining women and were now arguing about the ordination of gay and lesbian people. Underneath all the argument was the same set of basic questions over the changing roles of men and women and a whole set of arguments about authority. In addition, there was still a covert presumption that women were someone else's property instead of full human beings. And another presumption was still alive—that homosexuality was sin.

After the vote in the House of Bishops in September 1990, and after his speech in the House following the vote,

Jack Spong consulted, as he said in the sermon previously cited:

> With people at the highest levels in the House of Bishops, I was . . . encouraged to proceed with your [Barry Stopfel's] ordination to the diaconate. As a strategy, however, it was also suggested that I might ask Bishop Righter to preside over your diaconal ordination as a way of diffusing the negativity. It was the feeling of these leaders that this tactic would keep this ordination from being a media circus.

During the six-month period preceding Barry's ordination, I had, of course, been a part of meetings with the staff of the Diocese of Newark, with the Standing Committee of the Diocese, with Jack Spong, and with Barry himself. There was no doubt in my mind that Barry met every objective standard for ordination. His educational background was tops. Every examination or screening commended him to the bishop for ordination. Above and beyond that, Barry and Will lived as a family unit through the continuous questioning that the process required. Each had to cope with their sexuality and their future given the ferment in the Episcopal Church. They got through each day, only occasionally with gritted teeth, but more often with a lightness of spirit and a sense of humor. Both are very bright people. In serious discussions, they were, and are, articulate and compassionate. They are also filled with insight. They were, and are, faithful to the Gospel, as well as to each other.

There is no doubt that the oppressive nature of the national Episcopal debate affected each of them. Almost every day, I saw Barry in the diocesan office in Newark. He was at times discouraged, but he always maintained a future vision of hope. When Jack asked me to ordain Barry, I said, fairly easily, "Yes, I would be glad to." In saying those words, I was agreeing to ordain a qualified person to the diaconate. I was not making a revolutionary statement, although others interpreted it that way. I was not trying to confront the church with an ordination. I was not looking for a way to get the subject of gay/lesbian ordination considered. I was, instead, agreeing to ordain a person who had met all the tests every other person is expected to meet before ordination. In a sense, it was more than time for this ordination to occur, honestly and publicly.

On September 30, 1990, a beautiful fall evening, in the Church of the Atonement, Tenafly, New Jersey, on behalf of the Bishop of Newark and the people of the Diocese of Newark, I ordained Barry Stopfel to the diaconate, the first stage of ordination in the Episcopal Church. The church was full to overflowing with people from all over the diocese who had waited four extra months for this ordination. At the appointed time for objections, one solitary layperson stood up and read his objection. Since it was the kind of point that had been dealt with in almost every screening committee Barry had seen, I simply announced that the objection had already been heard by innumerable people and we would therefore go on with the ordination. At that point, the crowded church exploded with joy and applause. Barry was ordained the way every Episcopal deacon is ordained. It was a magnificent moment for all of us. Hardly any notice was taken in either the church or the secular press. Jack's advisers had been right: There was no media circus.

The next step for Barry was ordination to the priesthood. Again, the Presiding Bishop asked Bishop Spong not to schedule Barry's ordination to the priesthood until after the General Convention of the Episcopal Church in Phoenix, Arizona, in July of 1991. Imagine the pressure—on Barry, Will, and Jack Spong. It was almost inhuman. Three things happened at that convention in the House of Bishops on the subject of sexuality. First, there was an attempt to amend the canons of the Episcopal Church to prohibit the ordination of gay or lesbian people unless they took the vow of celibacy. The resolution seeking to accomplish that was called the Frey Amendment, after Bishop William Frey, the former Bishop of Colorado and dean of the Trinity School of Ministry in Ambridge, Pennsylvania. For reasons I do not understand, John Howe, Bishop of Central Florida, offered that resolution. It failed in the House of Bishops by ten votes. Second, there was an attempt to censure me for my ordination of Barry. My name was coupled with that of the Bishop of Washington, D.C., who had, in June of 1990, more than three months prior to my ordination of Barry Stopfel, ordained Elizabeth Carl, a lesbian who lived openly with her life partner. The resolution of proposed censure had both our names in it and sought censure on the basis that we had "violated the position of this church" as set forth in a 1979 resolution passed at the General Convention in Denver, Colorado, and also that we had violated the collegiality of the House.

The debate on that resolution of 1979 was confused. The resolution was a compromise resolution that used the language "not appropriate" in connection with ordaining a gay or lesbian person living openly with a partner of the same sex and *recommended* that such persons not be ordained. The language was chosen, after hours of discussion, in order to achieve passage—not to establish a teaching or a doctrine. John Coburn, the former Bishop of the Diocese of Massachusetts, had been president of the House of Deputies of the General Convention, and Hugh Jones, retired U.S. circuit court judge, had been a member of one of the key committees considering and framing the resolution. They are both colleagues of long standing with each other and with me. While still in seminary, I had served with John Coburn on the Province I College Commission. In 1970, I served with Hugh Jones on the General Convention Structure Commission. The memory of each is quite clear—the resolution in no way was meant to be definitive as doctrine. It was intended as a compromise resolution that would permit the convention to make a statement about sexuality. Very soon after the 1979 General Convention passed this compromise resolution, a group of twenty-one bishops, led by John Krumm, Bishop of the Diocese of Southern Ohio, signed a statement of conscience saying they could not abide by the resolution, even in its compromise form.

The people who presented me for trial over sixteen years later tried to rely heavily on this resolution. They claimed it represented "doctrine" and that I had violated it. Once again, our collective memory failed. My accusers tried to convert a compromise resolution into doctrine!

But in 1991 at the General Convention in Phoenix, there was still a lack of unanimity about the meaning of the 1979 resolution. And there was certainly no unanimity about the meaning of collegiality in the House of Bishops. The arguments about the proposed resolution of censure were far from uniform, as well. Walter Dennis, the Suffragan Bishop of New York, argued that the resolution of censure was inappropriate because we were, in the House of Bishops, lacking a "due process." Many bishops stood up and asked that their names be added to the censure document because they had ordained gay and lesbian people living openly with lifetime partners. The Bishop of West Texas, John MacNaughton, like many bishops before him who represented archconservative views about human sexuality, pleaded with the members of the House to give him something to take home. He wanted to satisfy people who were not at the convention but who were opposed to the ordination of gay persons.

At the meeting in Phoenix, another significant thing happened. We passed a change in our canons that seemed minor at the time. I voted for it because it seemed like a revision that might be helpful. The Bayne Report had asked that we adopt a canon requiring that two-thirds of the House of Bishops approve before a bishop could be tried for heresy. It was adopted. That canon had been in effect for a number of years. In 1991, in Phoenix, Bishop Wantland (later to be author of the presentment) moved, on behalf of Constitutions and Canons, that the two-thirds be changed to 25 percent. Looking back, one can see the possibility of a plan being hatched. By reducing the number of votes necessary, it would be much easier to get a trial.

In spite of all that, the results of the General Convention of 1991 were clear. Nothing was done to stop the ordination of Barry Stopfel. Bishop Spong called Barry from Phoenix before the convention ended. They set a date for his ordination to the priesthood.

I attended that service and it was a joyous occasion, just as the diaconate ordination had been. Along with all the priests who were present, I joined Jack Spong in the laying on of hands when that time came in the service. I had forgotten to pack a stole. When the time came to vest, Barry told me he had a stole he would loan me. It was a red one, studded with rhinestones! At the coffee hour afterward, I kept my vestments on instead of wasting the time it would take to change. Louie Crew came up to me, looked at me carefully from head to toe, noticed the red stole studded with rhinestones, the flowing red bishop's vestment and its white counterpart, and said with a twinkle in his eyes, "When I go to church coffee hours, I don't dress in drag! How come you do?" The lightness of that moment is expressive of the whole evening. Its solemnity was real and carried out beautifully by choir, congregation, acolytes, and assembled clergy. But it was a solemnity infused by Easter joy. Barry continued to serve as a priest and assistant to the rector at the Church of the Atonement, Tenafly, until shortly before he received a call to become rector of St. George's, Maplewood, New Jersey. Again, his qualifications and his relationship with Will stood out. The search committee of St. George's found him to be the best qualified of all the candidates they interviewed and his relationship with Will seemed the strongest and healthiest marriage of any of the candidates they interviewed—straight or gay.

IN AUGUST 1994, the General Convention met again, this time in Indianapolis. Again, we had arguments about sexuality. They were long-winded, with the Bishop of Fort Worth, Jack Iker, trying to reargue the issue regarding the ordination of women. The longer he went on, the more irate people became. We had, as the saying goes, "been there, done that." To reargue the case, without any kind of motion to speak to, was clearly out of order. At times, we are awfully tolerant of aberrant behavior. Advocates of women's ordination in the gallery could hardly contain their rage.

A special committee authorized by the 1991 General Convention, composed of bishops, clergy, and laypersons, had made a report about sexuality. The committee, aware of the fact that they would not have a finished report until time for publication in the preconvention papers, kept each draft of their report confidential. The existence of the committee and the work they were doing raised the anxiety level of the right-wing people so much that they went out of their way to find a way to create a storm of protest in midprocess. The committee worked hard and produced several drafts before they were ready to issue a final report. As the different versions were revised and reworked, they were reviewed by the House of Bishops; it was one of those versions that the conservatives leaked to try to discredit the committee. Ed Browning, the Presiding Bishop, got riled enough to issue a public letter to Episcopalians United, chastising them for intruding in what was meant to be a thorough and fair process, and for basing their intrusion on the version of the report that had been leaked to them when there had already been two more revisions of the report. Most of the members of the church were patient enough to wait until the report was released at the General Convention.

The bishops of Province VII (New Mexico, Kansas, Oklahoma, West Missouri, Arkansas, Louisiana, and Texas) were not that patient. They tried to anticipate what might be in the document, and then, by a statement they issued, they sought to contravene the processes of the General Convention. Before anyone except bishops had seen the report, based upon an outdated version of what the committee was producing, their statement was an attempt to tell people what their conclusions should be. The Rt. Rev. Sam Hulsey, Bishop of Northwest Texas, did not concur with the other bishops of Province VII in producing their statement. Displaying real Christian courage, which more and more people will appreciate as time goes by, Sam chaired the committee that designed and executed the extra meetings of the House of Bishops, seeking to build a collegiality that was almost nonexistent, one that would be real collegiality, not coercion to uniformity by a minority.

Some one hundred bishops signed the statement that the bishops of Province VII put together. The statement is called "An Affirmation in Response to the Proposed Pastoral of the House of Bishops Concerning Human Sexuality." A sample of its content is the following: "The fundamental element in Christian sexual morality is the discipline of self-control called Chastity, which means absolute faithfulness in marriage and sexual abstinence apart from marriage."

There were and are countless people in the Episcopal Church to whom the Province VII affirmation represented plain bad news. In view of the work that a committee had done to produce a study document that would permit the whole church to become engaged in a study of sexuality, the affirmation seemed to foreclose on discussion, offering a declaration in its place. Someone had to speak for and on behalf of thousands of others in the church as well as those we are constantly trying to reach who live outside the institution. That night, Jack Spong couldn't sleep. He stayed up until the wee small hours to write a statement he called "A Statement of Koinonia." The next morning, he read the statement to a member of the gay community and it brought tears to that person's eyes. It was read to the House of Bishops, by Bishop Spong, on August 25, 1994. It says, in part:

> We believe that sex is a gift of God.
>
> We believe that some of us are created heterosexual and some of us are created homosexual.
>
> We believe that homosexuality and heterosexuality are morally neutral, that both can be lived out with beauty, honor, holiness, and integrity and that both are capable of being lived out destructively.
>
> We believe that those who know themselves to be gay or lesbian persons, and who do

not choose to live alone, but forge relationships with partners of their choice that are faithful, monogamous, committed, life-giving, and holy are to be honored.

We also believe that the ordained ranks of the church are open to all baptized Christians and that through our regular screening process, we will determine who is both called and qualified.

We recognize that by canon law the choice of fit persons to serve in the ordained ranks of the church is not the prerogative of bishops alone, but of the whole church. We pledge ourselves to ordain only those persons whom the testing and screening process reveals to be wholesome examples to the flock of Christ. But, let there be no misunderstanding, both our lives and our experience as bishops have convinced us that a wholesome example to the flock of Christ does not exclude a person of homosexual orientation, nor does it exclude those homosexual persons who choose to live out their sexual orientation in a partnership that is marked by faithfulness and life-giving holiness.

We want this house and the whole church to know that we can be faithful to Christ and to our ministries as bishops in no other way than by affirming these principles.

With that statement, Bishop Spong restored a sense of balance to what we were doing and gave many of us in the House an opportunity to add our names to the "Statement of Koinonia." The statement gave to our church a sense of being in an inclusive church. I was one of seventy-two signers. My signature on that statement was cited by the bishops who presented me for trial for heresy as evidence of heresy.

Dr. Louie Crew points out in articles in both *The Witness* (November 1994) and *The Voice of Integrity* (Fall 1994–Winter 1995) that it is not enough to say that 71 bishops signed the Koinonia statement and 101 signed the Province VII statement. Dr. Crew says this: "Those who have endorsed Bishop Spong's statement are not marginal: they oversee forty percent of all Episcopalians. They also serve areas 5 percent more heavily populated than the areas served by those who signed the Province 7 document. By contrast, the Bishops of Province 7 have overseen the most dramatic decline of all parts of the Episcopal Church during the past two decades, in terms of percent of their local populations." He provides the following statistical data:

	No. of USA Dioceses	Communicants
Bishop Spong's statement	29	967,097
Prov. 7 statement	36	645,827
Neither statement	34	833,126
Totals	99	2,446,050

Crew's statistics helped to reinforce the sense of balance and sanity that the "Statement of Koinonia" inaugurated. I may mourn the absence of the leaders of the past in the current House of Bishops, but I also recognize that their leadership emerged in times different from ours. The church and the needs it must address are quite different from those of the 1950s, just as surely as the church of the 1950s differed dramatically from the church of the nineteenth century. In the language of the old hymn, "New occasions teach new duties, time makes ancient good uncouth."

Perhaps those "new duties" were what Ed Browning had in mind on the occasion of his election as Presiding Bishop at the 1985 General Convention in Anaheim, California, when he said, "There will be no outcasts in the Episcopal Church." Ferment as intense and frustrating as ours has been over the past forty years in the church also produces singular, striking moments of illumination.

CHAPTER 3

The Presentment

For more than forty years, the leaders of the Episcopal Church have been seriously engaged with inclusion. The following excerpt, from a foreword written by Ed Browning to *The Episcopal Church's History, 1945–1985*, describes clearly some of the events of those forty years:

> During these forty years, the Episcopal Church adopted a new Book of Common Prayer, a new Hymnal, voted to welcome women into the fullness of ministry as deacons, priests, and bishops. We've accepted the challenges and opportunities of the civil rights era, worked for peace with justice, and sought to open our doors to all seeking a new life in America. The progress in ecumenical relations during the latter part of the twentieth century is greater than at any other time since the Reformation. Not only have we witnessed the development of the World Council and National Council of Churches, the Epis-

55

copal Church has reached a number of milestones in its relationship with other denominations, resulting in bilateral covenants. Modern developments in communications and transportation have enabled us to establish closer ties with our Anglican brothers and sisters throughout the world. These "bonds of affection" have developed largely through the work of the Anglican Consultative Council which was established by the 1968 Lambeth Conference.

When Ed Browning made this statement at his election as Presiding Bishop in 1985, "There will be no outcasts in the Episcopal Church," he summarized forty years of history and a hope for the future. I was more than a bit surprised to hear the negative reaction to those words. Because of the previous forty years of history, I was amazed by the intensity of the reaction of various people from some parts of the country over the ordination of someone such as Robert Williams.

Earlier, in 1977, a similar kind of convulsion hit the House of Bishops when Paul Moore, the Bishop of New York, ordained Ellen Marie Barrett, an out lesbian, to the priesthood. His clear handling of her ordination appeared to have taken us to another level of inclusion. Even though there was a lot of excitement over Robert Williams's and Barry Stopfel's ordinations, inclusion, its terms and justifications, continued to be the focus of the Episcopal Church in the nineties. Jack Spong had joined Paul Moore as a courageous leader and had taken an enormous amount of flak as a consequence, including enough hate mail for a whole lifetime. So I was stunned and flooded with anger and incredulity when Ed Browning called me on the phone to tell me I was being presented for heresy.

On January 30, 1995, the phone call came before breakfast. Ed was at his retreat in central Pennsylvania. It was early enough in the morning so that Nancy and I had not had our coffee (or for that matter, our breakfast) yet. We were luxuriating in our house and its setting. On eight acres of a wooded, rocky New Hampshire hillside, our house is surrounded by evergreens of various sorts. It was still brand-new to us, as we had lived here for only a year and a half when the phone call came. Nancy had that day off. Winter was all around us, covering the ground with snow, embroidering the drooping branches of evergreens. Our year-old golden retriever, Phoenix, had already been outside and now bounded in, hopping up on the bed as I took Ed's call. The dog wanted me to play. But Ed's tone indicated that this would not be a playful day. The sun began to break through the trees, warming the house. And it got warmer when Ed told me the reason for his call. He said he had been notified by William Wantland, the Bishop of Eau Claire, Wisconsin, that he and nine other bishops were sending him an official presentment, seeking to have me tried for heresy. My first reaction was an angry and amazed "What for?" Ed said that was the same question he had asked Wantland when he heard about it. The letter to Bishop Browning from Bishop Wantland said, in part:

It is with great reluctance that we have taken this action. Further the fact that the action was filed against Bishop Righter is not a personal attack on him. Simply put, we are convinced that the Episcopal Church clearly teaches that it is not lawful or appropriate to knowingly ordain a practicing homosexual. We are convinced that Walter Righter did so. To ordain or to advocate ordination of a known practicing homosexual, or a heterosexual engaged in sexual relations outside of marriage, is contrary to the teaching of the church.

We have chosen to make this presentment against Bishop Righter because his action is the least recent such ordination within the current five year statute of limitation. Should this matter be set for trial, it is our intention to file Presentments against the next most recent offender, and so on, until we are current in bringing to trial all those who have knowingly violated the teaching of the church.

Then Ed explained that Bishop Wantland had said that he and the nine other bishops intended to proceed with presentments of the Bishop of Newark, John Shelby Spong; the Bishop of Pennsylvania, Allen Bartlett; the Bishop of Michigan, Stewart Wood; and the Bishop of Washington (D.C.), Ron Haines. Browning told me he had made it firmly clear to Bishop Wantland that the news of the presentment was his, the Presiding Bishop's, to release and not anyone else's. He asked me, on his behalf, to call those bishops and inform them that they were next on the list, according to his conversation with Bishop Wantland. Jack Spong, who had suffered enormous hostility because of his ordination of Robert Williams, and who was not happy about the way he had been treated (for good reason), said, "Walter, let the national church pay for it!" I had not asked for his help. His was an honest gut reaction. Ron Haines, Bishop of Washington, was driving his car around the capital when he got the message. In typical caring and pastoral response, he called me immediately on his car phone. He was concerned about the same thing that Jack Spong was concerned about. "How can you pay for it?" he asked. "What expenses do you envision? How are you feeling? What are you thinking?" Stew Wood, the Bishop of Michigan, had also suffered through an attempt to cite him for trial. It had been started from within his own diocese. In his case, in accord with the canon under which he was charged, a special committee was appointed by the Presiding Bishop from among the active bishops—to test the validity of the charges. They decided the charges were not valid. To be told it might happen to him again raised the possibility of double jeopardy.

All were as astonished as I was. We were all certain there was another agenda besides heresy—an agenda that had not become completely apparent to any of us yet. All expressed support. All suspected a coordinated effort—could it have been a conspiracy? Each of the bishops I talked to expressed a degree of cynicism about using a heresy charge to bring the issue, whatever it was, to a head. Allen Bartlett, the Bishop of Pennsylvania, with whom I had served on the Executive Council, gave the best response of any when he said, "That's a bummer!"

The only trial of a bishop for heresy the Episcopal Church had ever experienced occurred in 1923, when the retired Bishop of Arkansas was tried for saying that communism had supplanted Christianity. With today's medical knowledge, we now know he was suffering from senile dementia. Attempts to try active bishops had not succeeded. Was I singled out because I was retired?

I decided I had to inform the persons closest to me and most affected by this charge. Although my canonical residence is in Iowa, I live in the Diocese of New Hampshire, and I occasionally work in the Diocese of Vermont, the Diocese of Western Massachusetts, and the Diocese of Massachusetts. So I decided I should let Douglas Theuner, the Bishop of New Hampshire, and Mary Adelia McLeod, the Bishop of Vermont, know that a presentment was being made. It seemed to me I should also let my successor as the Bishop of Iowa, Chris Epting, know. I told our four children before the media could inform them. Three of them thought the idea of a heresy trial was not only ridiculous but also incomprehensible. The fourth, my daughter, Becky, who lives in Des Moines, is a marketing expert for a division of AT&T now spun off from the parent company and called Lucent Technologies. She has learned the value of brevity. She said, "Kick butt, Dad!"

I told one other group of people what was happening. Each Sunday, for several weeks, I had been taking services at the Gethsemane Church, Proctorsville, Vermont. It is a small group of people, hanging on to existence by a thread. It was easy to assume that they would be conservative on the issue of homosexuality. I was there on a Sunday, knowing that the following Monday the Presiding Bishop was publicly announcing the presentment. Because I had begun to bond with the people of Gethsemane, I thought that I had better tell them what they would read in the paper the next day. So I simply made an announcement. I wanted them to hear it from me. After the announcement, we continued the service with the celebration of Holy Communion. I remember wondering what their response would be at the door.

After the service, greeting the folks at the door was a marvelous experience. Vermonters can be terse and pointed. They were. But their comments were uniformly supportive, expressing a desire to have the church settle the issue on behalf of the gay/lesbian population. Some said, "I thought the church had settled this issue a long time ago!" Others commented, "A heresy trial—that's ridiculous!" One couple was puzzled by the issue and decided they needed to "read up" on it.

An older couple, easily in their mid-eighties, seldom said much except "Yep" on their way out the door. On a previous Sunday, Walter and Margaret Bixby had attended the coffee hour after the service. I was looking at the pictures of the previous bishops of Vermont that always hang in parish houses somewhere. As I looked at each picture, I pointed to it and asked them if they knew that person. Each question was answered with a "Yep!" When I got to the last picture, one of a man I did not know—Vedder Van Dyck—I said, "Did you know him?" Walter responded for both of them. He said, "Yep! Been around a long time, y'know." On the day of my announcement, it was ten degrees below zero outside. As the Bixbys walked by and shook hands, I said, "Bundle up; it's cold outside!" They both said, "Yep!" and then kept on moving. They did not go to the coffee hour that day. I did, staying for perhaps fifteen minutes, then gathered my vestments together and headed to my car. As I walked out of the door of the parish house, Walter and Margaret were standing there in the subzero weather. She said to me, in her Vermont accent, "Where's you-ah cah?" I pointed to my red Subaru wagon. Walter went over to it, opened the door, and said, "We waited for you, so we could open you-ah dooah for you!"

As I drove home, it occurred to me that the institution of the church is often far behind the intuition of its people. I was, and continue to be, grateful for that experience. It told me that the legislative processes of the church need to catch up to where the people's hearts and minds are. It told me to question my presumptions regularly and to remember people like Walter and Margaret Bixby while I am doing the questioning.

On Monday, February sixth, the Presiding Bishop mailed out copies of the presentment to the appropriate people. The presenters knew the mailing would take place February sixth, and from their point of view, they were then free to release the story to the media. And they did that with great fervor. A reporter named James Jones from the *Fort Worth Star-Telegram* was the first person to call. He had a copy of the presentment in his hand, and on his desk a copy of the legal brief the presenters had written. He wanted to ask me questions about my thoughts. Trouble was, I didn't have a copy and would not have it until late in the day on Wednesday. I was angry that he had been given a copy, obviously supplied by the office of the Bishop of Fort Worth, Jack Iker, and that I did not have one. So I strongly suggested he ask the Bishop of Fort Worth all the questions he had asked me, because I was not equipped with the information. The Bishop of Fort Worth had apparently paid no attention to the Presiding Bishop's word that the news was his (the PB's) to release.

I did the same thing with the reporter from the newspaper in Eau Claire, Wisconsin, who had been supplied information by Bishop Wantland. Her questions were the kind that Bill could answer as well as I could. It seemed more appropriate that his serenity be disturbed instead of mine. The thought struck me, as I calmed down, that Wantland and Iker were like exact copies of Jack Horner, who stuck in his thumb, pulled out a plum, and said, "What a good boy am I!" Self-congratulation made them want to share their work with the media as rapidly as possible. They seemed to have little sensitivity to how their actions invaded the quiet life Nancy and I had begun to build for ourselves. More particularly, my anger focused on Bill Wantland for being so cavalier, for his insensitivity to me and to the traditions of the House of Bishops. He had been a bishop long enough (fifteen years) to know better. I expected more of him than that.

I had known Bill Wantland for some years. I had supported his election as a bishop even though we differed greatly on most of the issues before the church. Like me, he had gone through a divorce and remarriage. I had some sympathy for what that felt like. Although we were never close enough, as associates in the House of Bishops, to share those feelings, I certainly expected him, as the leader of the ten presenters, to consult with me prior to bringing this charge. There had been no correspondence with me and no telephone calls. Yet, embedded in the policies and guidelines of the House of Bishops are words that clearly call for consultations.

Years before, as a parish priest in Nashua, New Hampshire, and as a bishop in Iowa, one of my jobs was to handle news releases correctly. Sometimes one had to discuss the issues with the media to make sure they got the story right. But this was the first time I had felt betrayed by my fellow bishops over the way in which they were handling information. Things were handled ineptly. Not only did I not have a copy of the papers I needed, because they were on their way from the Presiding Bishop's office, but the basic papers had already been released with a spin that was favorable to the accusers. They lacked the accompanying letter from the Presiding Bishop, which told of the process necessary to pursue the charges. Without this letter, the reporters were at a disadvantage, struggling with the accuracy of their coverage.

Initially, I wanted to be very cautious about what I had to say. I had been an ordained priest for forty-four years. Ten people were questioning, in my retirement, my faithfulness and my doctrinal purity. They were doing this without any attempt to communicate with me about it beforehand, a clear recommendation of the Bayne Report. Besides cautious, I was plain angry, not only about the charges against me but about the way hundreds (even thousands) of gay and lesbian folk were being scapegoated in the process.

Two other reporters called. They were more supportive, easier to deal with. One was a young man from Midland, Michigan, Steve Waring, who told me he had heard about the presentment from someone who had sworn him to secrecy, and he could not tell me who. The grapevine had begun. Without adequate and open channels in advance, information will find a way to get loose. Not only was Steve trying to put together a story for his paper, the *Midland Daily News*; he was a participant in the founding of a new diocese in the state of Michigan. We chatted about that and about what little I knew of what was happening. His father had been dean of the cathedral in Sioux Falls, South Dakota, while I was the Bishop of Iowa, a neighboring state. We had known each other during that time. I felt sure he would write something for the *Midland Daily News* and perhaps for the newspaper he was helping to start in his new diocese.

The second person to call, Jim Solheim, was from the Episcopal News Service. Again, he had all the papers and I did not, so I simply could not respond intelligently. Jim became a good friend in the next year and a half and I came to respect his work greatly. Many times, he gave me his ear and his advice about how to handle complicated information about the presentment.

At 4:00 p.m. on February eighth, my copies finally arrived. In the meantime, Jack Spong had called to tell me that his chancellor, Michael Rehill, would, on behalf of the Diocese of Newark, represent me throughout the proceedings. I had gotten to know Michael during my time within the Diocese of Newark. He is more than thoroughly steeped in church history and doctrine, deeply profound in his devotion to the church and his faith in God, exceedingly capable in both secular and canon law. I was delighted to hear he would represent me. The treasurer of the diocese, John Zinn, set up a special account called the Righter Defense Fund. The Rev. Jack Croneberger, rector of the Church of the Atonement, and Rudy Knolker, a member of Oasis, became cochairs of a national fund-raising effort for the support of my defense. Barbara Lescota, financial assistant to John Zinn, saw to it that I got regular reports of the receipts of that fund. An ad was taken out in the national newspaper of the Episcopal

Church, *Episcopal Life*, appealing for help. The Diocesan Council of the Diocese of Newark pledged its support. Most of the money raised went to pay Michael Rehill's fees. The amount of time he put into the case was enormous. A small portion of the money raised went to pay for our extra telephone bills, and mailing expenses. If more was raised than was needed, it was to go to the Presiding Bishop's Fund for World Relief. The Diocese of Newark was immensely supportive and remained that way throughout the entire process.

Paul Cooney, the chancellor of the Diocese of Washington, D.C., called me about the same time to ask thorough questions about my welfare, about my financial situation, about how Nancy and I were handling the shock of having my retirement invaded by an alien force. He, like his bishop, has a very pastoral heart. Paul, along with the chancellors of Pennsylvania, Michigan, and Chicago, formed a group with Michael Rehill to shape the words and strategy of my response. They came to be known as Bishop Righter's "dream team." They are all thoroughly committed to the Gospel message and extremely capable in the practice of law, and they kept our focus in the case clear and direct. We were ready. We were on "battle alert."

Nancy and I discovered, from the very beginning of this process, that humor helps you keep a sense of balance each day. When the presentment became public, we had been married a little over two years, and the process was to cause our relationship to intensify in ways that were beyond our control. We seldom talked about anything else. We went to bed late at night, after an evening spent at the word processor, dealing with letters that needed to be written and mailed, and as the pretrial hearing drew near, we needed to get up at 5:00 a.m. to welcome one of the major networks into our house as they prepared to videotape an interview.

Nancy now says there is nothing quite like having CNN in your living room. It even surpassed having the elephant that the church now had in its living room as a result of this case. We were about to experience a real test of our ability and our maturity as we went on the roller-coaster ride that God was calling us to. Both of us had been in marriages that were simply wrong for us. Both of us had spent the major portion of our lives in the Christian church. The institution and what it stood for was and is significant for us. But we needed the leavening effect of humor to get through the next fifteen months. And it began right away.

Nancy had been an active layperson in her parish in the Diocese of Long Island, especially in the Cursillo movement (a spiritual renewal program that began among Roman Catholics and spread to the Episcopal Church). As a social worker, she had also become active in AIDS work as the church tried to take its share of responsibility for the international crisis and epidemic that was affecting so many lives and families. We were doing our best to let our relationship with each other mature and deepen at a natural pace, knowing those qualities can only develop over time. The presentment altered that pace. After our marriage, in the fall of 1992, after my own Cursillo weekend, I happened to say to Jeff Smith, then lay director of Long Island Cursillo, that both Nancy and I were enjoying life in the New Hampshire woods. I added that both of us had had our share of difficulty in life and were looking forward to some peace and quiet. Jeff said, without a moment's hesitation, "If you were looking for peace and quiet, you married the wrong woman!" Nancy had become recognized and accepted within that Cursillo community as a liberal person. As a representative of the Brooklyn Episcopal AIDS Committee (BEAC), she and a comember attended a L.I. Diocesan Convention to raise consciousness about the presence of AIDS in our church. She took great delight in embarrassing friends by giving them condoms from GMHC (Gay Men's Health Crisis, a dynamic leader in AIDS-related work). We all laugh about the story, and it became a part of our family history. After the Presiding Bishop's phone call, and while Nancy and I were in the kitchen making coffee and toast, she gave me a hug and, with a twinkle in her eye, said, "If I was looking for peace and quiet, I married the wrong man!"

For all her humor, it was somewhat more difficult for Nancy to deal with the impact of the presentment on our lives. With a full-time job as a social worker, she often had to rearrange her schedule over the next fifteen months so she could fly off with me to someplace for an important event. Every day and most nights, we consulted, discussed, shared. Nancy now had two full-time jobs—social worker and wife of Walter.

In the few days immediately following the news of the presentment, we used humor as a tension reliever, and one of our best resources was Louie Crew. During one of many supportive phone calls, he said, "I'm sorry you are not going to be burned at the stake!" I told him I was not sorry about that but asked him why he was. He answered, "Because I just spent my life's savings on marshmallows!"

The canons of the church spell out a process that is to be used when a bishop is charged with heresy. It is a process unique to the Episcopal Church in the United States. Although we are part of the worldwide Anglican Communion, each church in every part of the world has its own identity. The presentment stirred interest in all kinds of places. I had mail from as far away as Moscow, Tangiers, and Hong Kong. But the process of the presentment and my defense is one that was developed by the church in the United States and is always in a state of evolution.

As we go on to consider the process, one needs to note

that two significant things emerged. As my accusers came forward, the tie between misogyny and homophobia became clearer and clearer. Each time I had voted (either in a real vote or a straw vote) for the ordination of women, the question of the ordination of gays and lesbians followed on its heels. My hope is that we in the Episcopal Church can now see that connection clearly etched in the names of my accusers, which included four people who still refuse to ordain women.

The second thing is of even greater significance. Despite the accusation of heresy against me, the onerous process the church had to deal with, and the cost of the stress and strain on Nancy and me, the process also revealed the profound change that is taking place in the attitudes of gays and lesbians and the profound sea change that is taking place in our society as it examines sexual roles and social contracts. I pray we in the Episcopal Church can continue to be responsible participants in that sea change, contributing to its evolution through work and ministry.

CHAPTER 4

"Don't Take It Personally"

In 1972, my first year as a bishop, in meetings of the House of Bishops I sat next to the vice president of the House, Robert Gibson, Bishop of Virginia, who seldom said a word. He had been a bishop for twenty-three years. I asked him how he managed to stay silent during the arguments that go on. With a grin, he replied, "I've been a member of so many committees and have heard most of the arguments, so I can tell how things are going to come out." Over the years, I found his wisdom helpful. If one had been on a committee that screened ideas before they got to the floor of the House, there seldom was a time when one heard a fresh argument on the floor that had not been previewed in the screening process—that is, until I was presented for trial. That process, begun by ten bishops, was not screened by any committee and came as a surprise to most of us. The secrecy involved in its conception and its execution, the possible connection between that and the action in Phoenix reducing the number of votes necessary for a trial from 66²/₃ percent to 25 percent, the sudden increase in the number of accusations against bishops for ordaining gay or lesbian persons who had same-sex lifetime partners, the orchestrated way in which the story was released to the press by the presenters—all pointed to a developing coup d'état.

The paper trail of the presentment started in January 1995. The House of Bishops met in March of that year at the Episcopal Conference Center in Kanuga, North Carolina. Ever since the General Convention of 1991, when an attempt was made to censure the Bishop of Washington, and me, the House has had an extra yearly meeting to focus on collegiality, not policy and procedure. The Kanuga Conference Center, owned by several dioceses in the southern part of the United States, managed well through the years, with finely kept grounds and buildings, good beds, and excellent food. Kanuga has played a central role in the Christian growth of hundreds of people. Set in the hills of North Carolina, near Asheville, it is reminiscent to me of the hills in the glens of Scotland. Kanuga could quite properly claim the title of "Queen of the Conference Centers." Many national conferences, as well as regional ones, have been held there over the decades.

March weather tends to be gloomy (as it might be in Scotland), and in 1995, it was rainy, with what I have learned to call "Scottish mist"—a little heavier than dew—which falls in the morning, much lighter than even a light rain. To encourage participation, the bishops were divided among tables of eight people each, with a chairperson, whose job was to keep us on the subject and to ensure that every person had a chance to have his say. I have many professional relationships within the House of Bishops, but few of those have extended to my personal life to include Nancy. The table I was assigned to had two exceptions. One was Don Hart, the former Bishop of Hawaii. He and his wife, Elizabeth, have remained friends of ours throughout this process. The other was Jack McKelvey, Suffragan Bishop of Newark, with whom I had worked in the Diocese of Newark. He and his wife, Linda, had become our good friends. Sam Hulsey, a "brother bishop" in the best sense of the word; Arthur Walmsley, retired Bishop of Connecticut (a judge in the Court for the Trial of a Bishop), FitzSimons Allison, retired Bishop of South Carolina, at whose feet I sat years before at the College of Preachers, immediately after his degree work at Oxford; Hunt Williams, Suffragan Bishop of North Carolina, whom I got to know better as a result of this table arrangement; Jim Coleman, Bishop of West Tennessee and one of my accusers; and John Chien, Bishop of Taiwan, made up the table I was assigned to.

There had been no advance notice of the presentment when the charge was actually made at the end of January. However, by the time of the meeting in March, there had been a lot of telephone conversations among individual members of the House, and a few group conversations as bishops got together for meetings. There was certainly no unanimity, and there definitely was a great deal of confusion. As we gathered, the Presiding Bishop, in his address, let people know he would not vote for a trial when the time came. He spoke eloquently against the idea of a presentment and a trial. That did not ease the confusion. The small table discussion got people talking. Almost at the beginning, with a burst of nervous energy, Jim Coleman said, "We don't want you to take this personally." Other members of the group sat there, awaiting my reaction. I could feel a clear rise in the tension level as people waited to see what I would say. I simply said, "That won't wash. When the history books are written, my name will be in them as the person accused of heresy by you and nine other bishops. That's pretty personal!" Not taking the issue personally would require splitting what God had made whole: my personhood and my belief and sense of principle.

During the free time, there was a lot of conversation about the presentment. During the week that we were gathered, many people worked hard to have the presenters withdraw their charges. One of the bishops asked the Bishop of Central Florida, John Howe, what it would take to get the accusation withdrawn. He replied, "Piece of cake!" When asked what he meant, he said, "If everyone in this House will promise not to ordain a noncelibate gay or lesbian person until the church makes up its mind about that, the accusation will be withdrawn." I was astounded when I heard such a manipulative tactic announced. Bishops trying to hold one another hostage? With me and the entire gay community as the price? Several times, the General Convention had refused to take the stand that Howe wanted. Essentially, he was proposing an "end run"—charges against me would be dropped if the bishops would agree to do what the General Convention had never agreed to do. In effect, the clergy and lay delegates to the General Convention were to be ignored in order to impose the will of the minority. Fascism, which I had spent three years of my life trying to defeat during World War II, had been revived—by bishops, and in the Church of God. Pretty desperate crowd, it seemed to me!

Yet our conversations also had a positive side. They triggered more formal conversations among people of opposing sides. Each evening in his room, Jack McKelvey brought together people who wanted to be supportive of me. All of them, in some way or other, were involved in conversations about dropping the presentment. It was quite clear from their reports that the presenters wanted to make a deal, that theirs was a "negotiable" position. There was one attempt at having semiformal negotiations. A group of my supporters came forward at one point and offered to meet with a group of those who favored the presentment in order to see what emerged. My supporters were the Rt. Rev. Jack McKelvey, Suffragan

Bishop of Newark; the Rt. Rev. Mary Adelia McLeod, Bishop of Vermont; the Rt. Rev. Jane Dixon, Suffragan Bishop of Washington [D.C.]; the Rt. Rev. Joe Doss, Bishop of New Jersey; and the Rt. Rev. Douglas Theuner, Bishop of New Hampshire. Representing the ten presenters were the Rt. Rev. Stephen Jecko, Bishop of Florida; the Rt. Rev. John David Schofield, Bishop of San Joaquin; the Rt. Rev. James Coleman, West Tennessee; the Rt. Rev. James Stanton, Bishop of Dallas; and the Rt. Rev. William Wantland, Bishop of Eau Claire. All ten were officially appointed by the Presiding Bishop as a group to seek some kind of agreement. But that group simply could not get started. The idea of a deal kept intruding in their discussion—a deal defined by someone outside of the group and offered to the group to adopt. Jack McKelvey told me later that a deal was introduced several times in the few hours of their discussion—by Stephen Jecko. Mary Adelia McLeod finally made an announcement on behalf of the five who were my supporters: It was simply that the bishops representing me were dropping out of any attempt at discussion. Nothing could emerge without dialogue, and that wasn't happening because this single idea of a deal kept intruding.

It was pretty obvious to any thoughtful person that the presenters had come to the conference prepared to offer a deal. Perhaps that was their intention from the very beginning: File charges in January and get the church all riled up; in March at Kanuga, we will get our way because no one wants a trial, especially of a bishop who has earned his retirement. That's probably what was meant by "We don't want you to take this personally." We don't want to have *you* tried. You're simply the "straw dog," the mechanism we're using to advance our point of view. Later that evening when I stretched my legs some by walking through the main building of the conference center, I encountered John Howe, the

Bishop of Central Florida and a leader among the presenters, who stopped me to tell me again that he and his associates did not want me to take the presentment personally. I tried to suggest to him that the action he and his associates had taken was so unusual that no one could divine their intention or motives. He refused to discuss that, saying he had only wanted to make the point that this was not a personal attack on me. I left him and walked outside, bumping into the Presiding Bishop as I went out the door. He stopped and said, "Are you all right?" I guess I must have come out of the door rather abruptly, with an angry look on my face. I nodded and said, "Yes, I came outside because I wasn't going to listen to any more of that bullshit." Sensing my anger and frustration, Ed said, "I'm glad you walked away." I deeply appreciated his compassionate response.

Keith Ackerman, the Bishop of Quincy, Illinois, and one of the ten accusers, wrote me a long note toward the end of the week, expressing real discomfort at the idea of the presentment and of his participation in it. He almost, but not quite, expressed a desire to have it withdrawn. He would continue to talk like that throughout the whole process, but the other nine accusers saw to it that he stayed in line. Keith and I had once served in the Diocese of Pittsburgh. I was a newly ordained priest; he was an acolyte in one of the parishes.

I had other personal, collegial relationships among my accusers. John Howe had been assistant rector at St. Stephen's, Sewickley, Pennsylvania, where I had spent my teen, U.S. Army, and college years. It was that parish that supported me in my quest to be a priest. It was from St. Stephen's that I went out to Rector, Pennsylvania, to start a new parish in 1947. My mother was a member of St. Stephen's, on the altar guild, and was buried from there. John Howe did not remember it, but he preached at her funeral, commending her for her Christian courage. James Stanton, Bishop of Dallas, had been a priest in the diocese of Iowa for five years while I was a bishop there. The people in his parish found him brilliant but intellectually lazy. We never had any serious arguments. In many ways, he was an innovator, but he could be insensitive. When we tried to raise $1.5 million for the poor and needy throughout the world and in Iowa, he was less than helpful. He wanted his parish to have a new organ. The Bishop of Texas, Ben Benitez, had served on the Executive Council of the Episcopal Church with me before he was elected Bishop of Texas. After he was elected, there were several times where we cooperated with each other, largely over clergy placement. The Bishop of Eau Claire, Wisconsin, Bill Wantland, had some people oppose his election as a bishop, and I tried to help overcome that opposition. His diocese was a near neighbor to Iowa. Some of our clergy went to his diocese to serve and some of his clergy interviewed in Iowa. We had always treated each other with regard and respect. At least so it seemed to me.

When it became clear that the presentment was a strategy to force a reversal on gay and lesbian ordination, using me as extortion, the members of my support group asked if I would be willing to make any kind of deal. I was firm. The General Convention of our church had refused again and again to say that gay men and lesbian women in committed relationships could not be ordained. These ten bishops were not only trying to get the bishops to do what the General Convention had never been willing to do, they were also seeking some way out of their self-inflicted marginalization and alienation. They were seeking to superimpose their will on the church. They overreached themselves. While this book was in an early stage of production, the story broke that Bill Wantland and some of the other bishops involved in the presentment were attempting yet another coup. It seems that beginning in August 1996 they secretly began establishing a nonprofit legal entity to parallel the Episcopal Church in the United States (ECUSA). Calling themselves the Protestant Episcopal Church in the United States of America (PECUSA), which just happens to be the form of the church's name used in its 1789 establishing constitution, the Wantland group registered this new corporation in twenty-five states "to engage in religious, educational and charitable activities and particularly the executive, administrative and financial administration of the Protestant Episcopal Church in the United States of America, otherwise known as the Episcopal Church. It shall have charge of the church pension fund and the church's program. . . ." The Presiding Bishop, Ed Browning, only a few weeks from his official retirement, said that ECUSA would explore all avenues, including legal action, if the new corporation is not dissolved.

Their target was really Jack Spong. For years, I had watched a fascinating scene play out. The Bishop of Newark takes seriously the necessity to speak to, and sometimes on behalf of, the disenchanted, the scientifically minded, the thoughtful maverick in our society who has walked out on the church. He calls them the "church alumni society." Every time he spoke about these disenfranchised in a public way, someone from the House of Bishops attacked him. It was a consistent pattern. I sat in discussion groups in the House at our annual meetings and listened to people sounding off about Spong and I got both angry and frustrated. In one group I was in, in Spokane, Washington, at the annual meeting of bishops held there, I was the only person in the group who thought Jack was very appropriate in his remarks. Intense intolerance for what he said was so alive in that small group, it was almost palpable. No matter what I said in his defense, it was dismissed rudely. One of the media people even suggested to Nancy that my ten accusers picked on me on purpose in order to deny Jack Spong the public forum he would have if they had accused him. He is articulate and can be devastating to his opponents. He is perhaps the brightest of all the bishops. His immediate response, if he had been accused, would have been withering. Perhaps that media person was right. At any rate, I am sure I was "in lieu of the Bishop of Newark." My accusers were willing to try to manipulate their Episcopal brethren even though the entire House of Bishops had subscribed informally to rules agreeing not to act or speak at the expense of another bishop.

The political nature of what was happening was clear. One of the bishops asked Jim Stanton, the Bishop of Dallas, why he had signed the charges against me. He said, "What have I got to lose?" Not exactly a statement of principle. At one of the evening support sessions in Jack McKelvey's room, we were trying to make sense out of what was happening. Looking at me, Jane Dixon said, "We may have to go to trial, and you may have to say so!" The minute she said that, it made perfect sense. It was the clearest way out of the confusion we were in. We had been seeking a political solution, which is exactly what my accusers wanted us to do, hoping they could wear us down by threat and by simply saying over and over again what their terms were for withdrawal of the presentment. We needed to couch our reply in principles, not politics. So I agreed to make my first speech in the House of Bishops in twenty-three years.

For me, there was another, deeply troubling issue at Kanuga. A critical point in our Eucharist service is the Exchange of the Peace. It follows the confession and precedes the prayers of the Communion service. At that point, the ministers and people are encouraged to greet one another, and this is done with a verbal exchange of "Peace" and a handshake, and sometimes a hug. The spirit in which this is done is one of clearing the air among participants. The New Testament is quite clear: If any person has anything between him or her and another, let the person clear it up before going to the altar with that other person to receive Communion. At Kanuga, we were at a meeting of 180 bishops. We would be eating all our meals together. We would be talking with one another in formal sessions and informally as we walked the grounds of the conference center. We would also have frequent celebrations of Holy Communion. In each celebration, there would be an Exchange of the Peace. I did not feel, as the meeting began, that I could do that with spiritual honesty with my ten accusers. They were attempting to dishonor my ministry. They had thrown a heinous label at me because it might conceivably serve their purposes to do so. I did not feel able simply to say, "The peace of the Lord be always with you" to any of them.

In search of some clarity for my discomfort, I sought out the chaplain to the House of Bishops, the Rev. Martin Smith, head of the monastery of St. John the Evangelist in Cambridge, Massachusetts. He was profoundly helpful. As we talked together, some things became obvious. It would probably take almost a year and a half for the presentment to play itself out. I did not want to stay away from Holy Communion while the House of Bishops was gathered. I could not let these ten people push me away from the Eucharist. To cope with what was happening, I needed the grace and strength I deeply believed came to me through the Sacrament. The reality of all of this had to be faced and I needed to let the ten presenters know how I felt. I did. I tried to do this as reasonably and peacefully as possible. Nonetheless, I am sure that something more than reason and peace was apparent. I was distressed and angry. I was deeply disappointed to find such machinations in a group of leaders of the church, supposedly mature individuals. I'm sure as I communicated those feelings, what I came up with was not an ideal solution. But it let me go to the Eucharist. It let me participate in the Exchange of the Peace with some of my ten accusers. We all understood that was being done in the midst of unresolved conflict among us—a conflict that church process was going to work out. My impression was that this was not as serious an issue for any of my accusers as it was for me. But this resolution permitted me to say to the Bishop of West Tennessee, "I must tell you what this action of yours and your nine other compatriots has done. And I must tell you in order to be able to continue to receive the Eucharist with you. And I hope you will tell the other nine for me."

In addition to my issues, there was another dynamic in play at Kanuga. Four of my accusers had still not agreed to ordain women, even though the church had endorsed that action in 1976—nineteen years before the charges brought against me. In that intervening time, we had ordained a large number of women, and we had had several women elected to the episcopate. The first, Barbara Harris, Suffragan Bishop of Massachusetts, was scheduled to celebrate the Eucharist while we were together. She is an effective, dynamic person, charitable to a fault to those not accepting of her, and a major source of strength, not only to the House of Bishops, but to the church itself. At that particular service, there were bishops, a dozen or so, who simply would not receive the Eucharist from Barbara because they did not recognize her as a valid priest or bishop, simply because she was a woman. When the time came to receive, however, one of the most ardent opponents of the ordination of women, the retired Bishop of Northern Indiana, the Rt. Rev. W. C. R. Sheridan, did receive. His small group of friends pounced on him after the service, asking why. His response, as described to me by someone who heard it, is classic. He said, "Charity overcomes scruples!" Prophetic words about life—not just the ordination of women.

FROM RESEARCH that my brother has done, which is not complete, it seems that my ancestor Peter Righter came to this country for reasons of conscience. Ever since then, it seems that each generation of our family has had its conscience stretched. My great-grandfather sued the city of Philadelphia because he felt they had exceeded the limits of eminent domain in taking some of his land. He had fought in the Civil War and he felt his service was being cheapened by the behavior of government. My grandfather was asked by Judge Elbert Gary to move from Philadelphia to Indiana to build the new mill and the new city to be called Gary, Indiana. But he felt, in good conscience, he could not sacrifice his family and his time with them in order to build a mill and city. He knew it would consume years of his life, taking all his waking hours each day. So he refused, for personal, conscientious reasons.

My father had a more dramatic event. When I was four years old, he took me with him to a part of Philadelphia where tough people lived. He was doing some work in the evening, as an accountant, that put him in touch with what we would call the Mafia these days. We rode in his Model T Ford coupe. He parked the car and we started to walk toward the business. Suddenly, he picked me up, put me inside a tailor shop, and then walked to where two men were fighting. He stopped the fight, took a pistol away from a man who was about to shoot the other man, and held them there until a policeman came and arrested them. Then he came to the tailor shop, took me by the hand, and we resumed our walk.

My brother, at the age of sixteen, had a job as an usher

in a theater. He was told by the theater owner that black people were to be seated in the balcony. He refused to do that and quit his job as a way of bearing witness to his own conscientious objection to what was going on. While I was in World War II and had my share of "doing my duty," I had never been faced with dramatic decisions and moments of resisting like those of my brother and forebears.

But here I was—at a House of Bishops meeting, at the age of seventy-two, seeing quite clearly, without hesitation, that I must stand up and say to the members of the House that we must have a trial. It was imperative, the only way to get initiative back in the hands of the House—and out of the hands of my accusers. So, among other words, I said, "The only way we can find out that a trial won't work is to have a trial!" I also relayed to them the story of the older couple from Proctorsville, Vermont, concluding by saying, "I don't want to bring the House of Bishops to the Bixbys; I want to bring the Bixbys, their kindness and wisdom, to the House." My twenty-minute speech was followed by a standing ovation. I had a sense that my willingness to stand trial had relieved the whole House of their inability to cope with the situation. Many bishops continued having personal conversations with my accusers, trying to find a way to drop the charges. My accusers, and their adherents, continued to have meetings and conversations. But their tactic had been defused. One bishop, Alden Hathaway, Bishop of Pittsburgh, stood up in a plenary meeting and said, "All we can do now is pray."

After my speech, the necessary events of the meeting continued. We left the Kanuga Conference Center on our way to more than a year of proceedings toward a pretrial process and a trial. For the second time in her history, the Episcopal Church was now to become preoccupied with the subject of heresy. In 1923, the subject was heresy. In 1995, the issue was again heresy. The hidden agenda was power.

The accusers were, from my point of view, the ones out of touch with reality—the reality of intimacy and of God's compassion and love and forgiveness.

My accusers, not understanding the tides of history and focusing only on their own fears, were attempting to stop the efforts of the church at inclusivity. In the 1950s, the Church Insurance Company (an Episcopal agency) offered each Episcopal Church in the United States (about seven thousand) free signs to put upon roads leading to each church. The red-white-and-blue signs gave the name and address of the local church and said THE EPISCOPAL CHURCH WELCOMES YOU. My accusers were alienated from the welcoming mission of the church. Some felt marginalized and wore their feelings like a badge of honor. They stepped out of the tide of history. For whatever reason, they could not stand the tension and the danger of living in the present. They tried to limit those whom we could welcome.

We all exist, all the time, on a fault line between the past and the future. The fault line is the present. It always has a sense of danger about it. It has a sense of excitement about it, too. It is where real life is lived. It is where we face the future with hope and faith. Much is unpredictable. Instead of moving toward the future with hope, my accusers sought to take the church backward into a time that seemed more secure to them.

In choosing the method they did—to accuse a fellow bishop of heresy and then use that accusation in an attempt to pressure the leaders of the church into accepting their agenda, they showed their bully mentality. The Episcopal Church has always thrived on discussion and ambiguity. You cannot have either when you seek a court decision through the use of canon law and serious charges such as heresy. After the meeting at Kanuga in March of 1995, the process was set. The accusation against me was no longer a bluff in order to force three hundred grown men, a sizable number of whom had lived productive lives and had retired, to do what a small minority wanted and had been denied several times by the major legislative body of the church. The Presiding Bishop was required, by the canons of the church, to continue the process, to determine if a trial should take place. And my ten accusers, like me, were to be judged by their peers as to the rightness and righteousness of their ideas. The attempted "coup d'état" was not over, but it had been, for the moment at least, defanged. The chaos and confusion had begun to give way to some shape and order. The initiative seized by the ten surprised not only the Episcopal Church but surprised the mainline churches in the United States, as well. During the process, I heard from ordained and laypersons from all the mainline churches in the United States. Jewish rabbis and Roman Catholic bishops wrote letters of support and sent personal funds for my defense. The initiative of my accusers had now given way to the initiative required of the Presiding Bishop by the canons of the church.

We were beyond negotiation. The bishops would either vote for a trial or against a trial. Seventy-six bishops— 25 percent of the House of Bishops—were needed for a trial or the whole thing would be canceled. Before the vote could be taken, Michael Rehill was to prepare a brief on my behalf, which responded to the charges of my accusers. That, along with the brief prepared by Bill Wantland, had to be mailed to each bishop, active or retired. After reading both, each bishop was expected to decide if there should be a trial. If they decided there should be one, they were to write the Presiding Bishop and say so. If they decided there should not be a trial, they were to do nothing—in effect, a negative vote. If the vote was for a trial, then we would begin work with the Court for the Trial of a Bishop. Their decision, if it involved imposing a sentence of any kind on me, would then have to be approved by two-thirds of the House of Bishops or it could not be imposed. It would take months of process, but it would give some clarity.

As I got on the bus at Kanuga to ride to the airport, I found a quiet peace welling in me about the events of the conference. I had come not knowing what to expect. I had had good reunions with many of the bishops who were longtime professional associates. Lots of retired bishops, as well as bishops I had never met before, came and expressed support for me. I had made my first and only serious speech in that House in twenty-three years, and it had moved us from being stuck in the manipulative mire created by fear of the future toward some clarity. At the airport, as I waited around for my flight to be announced, those of us who were there had a chance to engage in conversations about our families, about the practice of "bishoping," about the way the world was going, even about the national debt! Even though I had talked to her each evening, I looked forward to getting home to Nancy and our house in the woods, and our golden retriever. This was a good time to be alive. And God is good. Both convictions were clear to me as I soared toward New Hampshire.

CHAPTER 5

The Dilution of
Leadership

A BISHOP'S JOB is to keep his church family on the firing line of the world's most desperate needs and to learn to accept the exquisite penalty of such an exposed position."

John Elbridge Hines spoke those words while he was still the Bishop of Texas in 1963, prior to becoming the Episcopal Church's twenty-second Presiding Bishop. His professors at Virginia Theological Seminary led him to an understanding of the social implications of theological belief and he was taught the application of those beliefs in the beginning years of his ministry by the Bishop of Missouri, William Scarlett. John Spong, who always described John Hines as his closest friend, characterized his ministry as Presiding Bishop this way: "In his mind, a church that did not engage these issues [the Vietnam War, racial tension, poverty, urban decay] would die of irrelevance." Bishop Hines understood the development of and had a profound appreciation for the history of the Episcopal Church. He helped make some history himself. He recognized that huge social and theological changes were taking place and he did his best to keep the church family on the firing line with regard to the world's most desperate needs. He insisted we put our money and our strength where our creedal mouths were. Again, to quote John Spong, "He shaped the life of this church more dramatically than any single person in this century. He led us all beyond the limits of our fears into countless new frontiers."

John Hines is an example of the kind of person who became a bishop in this church in a generation that has almost passed from view. Sometimes, even the most ordinary priest in those times, when elected to the episcopate, grew to greatness through the nature of the task before him. The challenge of keeping the church family on the firing line would result in either leadership or failure.

From the time I became interested in church history, I heard people talk about a man named Samuel Seabury, who was our first bishop in the Episcopal Church. Rector of a church on Long Island, he was elected by a small group of clergy in Connecticut and sent to England to be consecrated and to return to this small church in the newly formed United States. English bishops, still sensitive about losing the American Revolution, refused to take a chance on consecrating someone from the rebellious colonies. So Seabury went to Scotland and was consecrated there by three Scottish bishops in the city of Aberdeen in 1784. Overlooked most of the time in this story is this: By returning to the United States, Samuel Seabury became the first bishop the Anglican Communion sent outside of the British Isles to work. In the more than two hundred years since that time, we have grown from a small provincial church to a worldwide communion that is a significant part of the Christian mission throughout the world.

The more than a thousand bishops in the worldwide Anglican Communion gather once every ten years at something called the Lambeth Conference. Started in the middle of the nineteenth century by the Archbishop of Canterbury to give the bishops a chance to talk with one another about the work they were doing and to look ahead, the first conference was held at the Archbishop of Canterbury's London residence, Lambeth Palace—hence the Lambeth Conference. Even though Lambeth Palace is a sizable place, it is much too small to accommodate more than one thousand bishops and their spouses today. The conferences in recent decades have been held at Kent University in Canterbury, England. Bishops still pool their dioceses' insights about mission and ministry, they still share their thoughts about the future, they study the Bible in small groups of ten persons, and they worship together in both small and large groups. It is truthful, I think, to say they pool their experiences, their hopes, and their prayers. They represent all races. They come from almost every country, certainly from every continent.

Just as the church grew and bishops' numbers and responsibilities changed from Samuel Seabury's time to John Hines's time, so the role of the bishop continues to alter after John Hines.

The man who followed Hines as Presiding Bishop gives us a good contrast. John Maury Allin was Bishop of Mississippi from 1961 (coadjutor) to 1974, when he became the twenty-third Presiding Bishop. Long before he was elected to the office of Presiding Bishop at the General Convention in 1973 at Louisville, Kentucky, he became a person who pushed for changes in the way things were being done in the Presiding Bishop's office. He did not push hard at all for changes in our society, as John Hines had done. Rumor had it, long before he was elected, that he wanted to be Presiding Bishop, and that his desire was evident in the way he behaved in the annual meetings of the House of Bishops. He was installed in the National Cathedral in Washington, D.C., the traditional place for our Presiding Bishop's seat, in 1974. As we gathered to process into the nave of the cathedral, I happened to be standing close to a woman from Mississippi, who was also in the procession. I asked what her diocese was like. She responded quite openly: "For the last ten years, it's been pretty sleepy, but now we've got Duncan Grey elected, I think we'll find some new life!" I looked toward the altar and said, "We're going in there to install your former bishop as Presiding Bishop of this church. Do you understand what you're saying?" Her response was, "I certainly do!"

In 1970, when I was a member of the General Convention's Structure Commission, my assignment was a subcommittee named the Executive Function, which included the office of Presiding Bishop, the Executive Council, and the national staff. I attended a meeting of the Executive Council simply to observe. The meetings were held in a beautiful setting in Greenwich, Connecticut, at a place called Seabury House. It was a large house with enough bedrooms and baths for the entire Executive Council. On the grounds was a smaller house, in which the Presiding Bishop and his family lived. It was in the formal dining room of Seabury House where I first met Bishop Allin, there for an Executive Council meeting. We sat across from each other and shared casual conversation until he discovered I was there as an observer for the Structure Commission. He stated quite clearly what he thought we should do with the role of the Presiding Bishop. However, the Structure Commission did not embody his suggestions in their report. Before he became Presiding Bishop, I was elected Bishop of Iowa (1971), and in 1973 he was elected Presiding Bishop. I was fascinated to see him redefine and implement the changes he had originally suggested to me in that brief supper-table conversation. His focus was on access, pulling the Presiding Bishop into frequent, regular touch with the provinces. At the same time, he did not have the great overarching vision of Bishop Hines. Bishop Hines's urging that we empower people who were marginalized or oppressed embodied a worldwide awareness that included the beginning of the pressure on American business to stop supporting the policy of apartheid in South Africa. Bishop Allin, by contrast, coped with a church that had a new prayer book (which he was lukewarm about), a church that was committed to ordaining women (which he opposed), and a church he described on the day of his election as a "ragtag army," not a church that could be described in the words of "Onward, Christian Soldiers" as marching in lockstep "like a mighty army." More than once, I heard him say we were a minority church with a majority complex. In more recent speeches, he has described the church as systemically ill. His defensiveness left little room for any overarching theological vision and encouraged those who shared his negativism to circle their wagons.

I served on the Executive Council of the Episcopal Church for six years while he was Presiding Bishop. At the first meeting I attended, I questioned, very directly, a proposal meant to expand the scope of the way the Presiding Bishop's fund for World Relief raised funds. It was obvious that my line of questioning was not welcome. It probed matters that Milton Wood, the Presiding Bishop's assistant, did not want studied. For six years after that (1979–1985), my assignments were minimal. Paul Chalk, a layman from Nevada, asked me to propose something about which he felt strongly. When I asked him why he did not propose it himself, he said, "If I do, I'm afraid the PB won't give me the committee assignment I would like." Bishop Spong described Bishop Allin as "chosen in reaction to dramatic and stretching leadership," who would "return our church to its path of risking nothing while claiming a new, benign piety."

In these two differing approaches to leadership, one

can see not only the alterations in the role of Presiding Bishop but also the complexities involved in the attempt to have me presented for heresy. The John Hines years, marked by social action, liturgical reform, and geographic outreach, generated intense excitement and sometimes equally intense misunderstanding and anger. John Hines's successor tried to calm the waters; he looked to his natural constituency, the South, for support. Even though Hines was himself a southerner, the South felt betrayed by him. Those southern bishops who felt enmity toward Hines's ministry and leadership style were only too glad to be placated by John Allin.

Allin's brand of leadership, concerned as it was with reconciling and placating, turned the House of Bishops into the Hall of Compromise. On every major issue, it was thought, we needed to compromise. It never worked. Once we had devised language that satisfied people, something happened to raise the issue again. Then we would struggle again over the same ground. Efforts to compromise produced more tension than reconciliation.

Tension of this sort peaked in what we may call "the Pike years." During the late fifties and sixties, James Pike, the Bishop of California, was a magnificent apologist for the Christian faith as well as for the Anglican Communion. Trained as a lawyer, then as a priest, college chaplain at Columbia University, dean of the Cathedral of St. John the Divine in New York City, he had a mind more alert, creative, and active than had been seen in a generation. Not surprisingly, some accused him of being a heretic or a communist. And not surprisingly, many of those accusations came largely from the South, as did the majority of accusations directed at John Hines and the major thrust of heresy charges against me.

Bishop Pike raised the issue of doctrine. Bishop Hines brought to the fore issues that concerned helping the poor, civil rights, and prayer book revision. In John Allin's time, the issue was the ordination of women. In Bishop Browning's time, the issue was sexuality, with a focus on homosexuality and its relation to the church. The common denominator underlying all the specific issues was the church's response to justice for all people.

To lead as John Hines did was, as he said, "to accept the exquisite penalty of an exposed position." Such exposure was precisely what the House of Bishops now sought to avoid, substituting for it something to take home with us, something designed not to rock the boat. Appeasing the laity only strengthened the hand of the conservatives and offered obstacles to a clear understanding of how communities of faith must lead, witness, and respond to a changing world.

Anxiety about the future gave birth, in the late eighties, to the Episcopal Synod of America and a group called Episcopalians United. While the Episcopal Synod focused its efforts again and again on blocking the ordination of women, Episcopalians United focused its efforts on the literal interpretation of the Bible. Both groups attracted members who were unhappy about the "new" prayer book. Both groups made a variety of threats, each of which hinted at "secession"—for example, withdrawing financial support from the national office and Bishop Browning's leadership. Negativism was their common bond. In fact, at the General Convention in Phoenix in 1991, they announced, through the voice of John Rodgers, a clerical deputy from the Diocese of Pittsburgh, that they would disobey any action of the church with which they disagreed.

One of the clergy who supported this new brand of evangelicalism was John Guest, who became rector of St. Stephen's Church, Sewickley, Pennsylvania, the parish church so close to me. St. Stephen's became a church that disregarded decisions made by the General Convention. For example, I attended services there one Sunday after we had adopted our 1979 version of the Prayer Book and found nothing but 1928 versions in the pews. An arrogant disregard of the work of thousands of clergy and laypeople in developing and using new worship forms made my worship experience that Sunday distasteful. St. Stephen's, once a leader in the Episcopal Church's work, became instead a church frozen in the past and thus unable to abide by the decisions of the General Convention, which was grappling with a changing reality. Further, Guest wanted to start a new seminary to represent and teach his brand of evangelicalism. He was prevailed upon by both Jack Allin, then Presiding Bishop, and Bob Appleyard, then Bishop of Pittsburgh, to endow a chair in one of our existing seminaries. But John Guest would not consider that option. As a result, we now have a seminary, Trinity School for Ministry, near Pittsburgh, that does not grapple with twentieth-century biblical scholarship, but it is graduating significant numbers of people who are entering the ordained ranks.

Fundamentalism as a threat is, of course, not confined to the House of Bishops or to the Episcopal Church. We have seen its seductions in other denominations and other world religions. It espouses a simplicity, appealing but dangerous, in that it reduces complex, multilayered issues to one-dimensional response.

During the 1970s, most educational institutions, religious and secular, drastically altered their curricula. Required courses in history, classical literature, scriptural tradition, and philosophy were replaced by multiple options, and courses examining current events, gender studies, and alternative traditions became increasingly common. There is much that is fresh and invigorating about that transition. But it is also true

that now, twenty years later, some people elected to the episcopate are untrained in the philosophical, rational, and spiritual traditions that undergird the Christian worldview. Some
have chosen instead a kind of fundamentalism to give them an
anchor.

Another factor, besides the way in which clergy are
educated, that affects the quality of membership in the House
of Bishops, can best be described with a story from my child-
hood. When I was three years old, my father got me a small
electric train for Christmas. It was supposed to be a surprise
from Santa Claus, but I heard it running on Christmas Eve
and got up out of bed and went downstairs, where I found my
father playing and tinkering with it. The next morning, it was
great fun. It was on a circular track around the Christmas tree
and it created great excitement for a three-year-old. For two
Christmases, it was a great addition to our Christmas tree. All
it did was run around the tree on the circular track. None of
my friends had one, so I always had a playmate in our house at
Christmastime simply to watch that funny little train.

When I was five years old, I came downstairs on
Christmas Day and found my little train gone. In its place was
a huge platform with the largest toy electrical train available
at the time. It was on tracks that had switches, electrical crossing signs, gravel roads made of fine gravel glued in place, a
railroad station, freight cars, and passenger cars with lights in
them. All I had to do to get everything working was to move a
little handle on a transformer. The train began to move, a
light went on in the model station, the crossing sign came
down across the gravel road, and the switches were ready to
be changed—it was an enormous gift for a five-year-old. It
took me years to catch up. It was from my grandfather, who
made the platform and assembled the equipment on it.

I don't think either my father or my grandfather ever

realized the competition that those two train sets symbolized. My grandfather was competing with my father for my attention and affection. At the same time, my father simply could not confront his father with what was going on. It took my father years, extending long after my grandfather's death, before he could be his own person. When praising my brother or me, often he would speak of how proud our grandfather would be of our accomplishments, when what we really wanted was *his* endorsement. Professionals call this, I think, self-differentiation. It is essential to one's self-esteem and ability to act decisively in various life situations. In spite of psychological examinations, and countless interviews on the way to ordination and eventually to the episcopate, there are many bishops who have not developed in their emotional and psychological growth. When they run into tough laypeople who threaten them with loss of funds, or even a regional culture that cannot understand the role of the church as a redemptive agent of change, those bishops either collapse or conform to the culture, instead of trying to lead it into transformation.

I must say at the same time that there are probably two-thirds of the active members of the House of Bishops who hold Scripture, tradition, and reason to be significant in the traditional Anglican manner. Approximately the same number are people who have a strong sense of self-differentiation. But there are still, even though a minority, approximately a third who do not have the capability of standing up to the kind of threats that some clergy and laypeople will make. They are not to be pitied or condemned, but they need the support and guidance from the rest of the House. That support, however, needs to be conditional upon their willingness to lead. Others speak up but insist that their point of view is the one that must be accepted by everyone else. When they go home, they say, "Well, you see, I said the right things at the national meeting, but they won't listen, so we'll have to go it alone." I think it is clear where that will lead—to marginalization and alienation. It leads to funds withheld unless everyone does things the way that particular diocese wants them done.

I have been a member of the House of Bishops for twenty-five years and have witnessed its struggles and challenges. If the Episcopal Church is to engage what John Hines terms "the world's most desperate needs," it seems imperative that we become more attentive to education and the proper selection of our bishops. Insecurity and divisiveness can stall even the most crucial change. The church deserves leadership that is up to the task: clearheaded, well-educated, decisive, and compassionate human beings who can speak their conscience and listen with open minds and hearts to others.

CHAPTER 6

Hartford

W<small>HILE</small> <small>I</small> <small>WAS</small> <small>IN</small> <small>SEMINARY</small>, and during our study of the history of heresies, I had a bull session with a friend, Louis Hirshson, who was the dean of Christ Church Cathedral in Hartford, Connecticut. Louis had been my rector, in Sewickley, Pennsylvania, through my teen, army, and college years. A graduate of Harvard, a businessman before becoming a priest, he had a keen and probing mind. He surprised me by saying, "Every preacher commits heresy every Sunday when he preaches." Louis, later president of Hobart and William Smith Colleges, was no slouch as either a scholar or a preacher. The thought of this bright, often caustic and sassy person committing heresy every Sunday gave me pause. Noting my surprise, he went on to explain: "Heresy, by definition, is partial truth. No preacher ever preaches the whole truth on Sunday morning. He doesn't have time. So every sermon is a part of the truth."

My brother, Richard, an architect by profession but an avid reader by avocation, had his curiosity aroused by the talk of heresy. He is seven years younger than I am, and he was incensed that his big brother was being accused of heresy. When I told him the nature of the charges, he said, "What happened to the primary message of the church—love and forgiveness?" He had not been an active church person since his midcollege years. But he had not lost the core of the faith. As the pretrial process went forward, he read up on heresy and sent me the results of his research. I was particularly struck by observations Arno Borst makes in his book *Medieval Worlds*.* Heresies in the Middle Ages "formed and spread because the Catholic Church would listen to new religious demands only hesitantly, or within the community of clerics. Under these conditions, heresies became the active, radically progressive wing of a religious movement that would usually enter into the church at some later point anyway." He cites, as a case in point, a Bishop Wazo of Liège in the middle of the eleventh century. The bishop was asked what should be done with heretics and he answered that God had patience with sinners; therefore, he would let the tares grow together in the field with the wheat until the last day. In the bishop's own words, his office was "not to bring death, but to give life." Karen Armstrong, author of *A History of God* and *Jerusalem*, wrote a piece for the *New York Times* as the Court for the Trial of a Bishop was convening in Wilmington for the first time in March of 1996. "History shows that heresy trials are largely fueled by a church's anxiety over challenges to its authority and social change."† She pointed out that heresy trials often reflect the larger society's struggles and look for enemies that do not exist. Both positions cast perspective on my presentment. Borst would see my decision

*Arno Borst, *Medieval Worlds* (Chicago, 1996), p. 99.
†Karen Armstrong, "The Episcopal Inquisition," *New York Times*, February 2, 1996.

to move forward with the trial as having its logical roots in "heresy" as the Middle Ages understood it, a move designed to force change or transformation in the face of our stalled church. Armstrong emphasized that the attempt to try me simply reflected the church's historical anxiety over social change that was challenging to its own authority.

The Bayne Report, which I referred to earlier, pointed out that the idea of a heresy trial in our time, in this part of the world, simply does not fit the realities of the day. A friend called me one day to remind me that heresy was meant to be the ecclesiastical equivalent of treason in a world where the divine right of kings was the paramount belief about the political system. In a world where democracy has been the paramount political belief (especially in the United States), heresy has no relevance. Perhaps that is why my accusers disclaimed the use of the word. Perhaps that is also the reason it does not appear in our canons. A dictionary definition of the word *heresy* does, however, embrace the language used by my accusers and the language of our current canons. My attorney and his advisers, the chancellors of several major dioceses, and several volunteer priests chose the word carefully to make it possible to describe the collective charges against me with one word instead of several.

I began to think of Louis Hirshson's "partial truth" and decided that heresy as partial truth is engaged in by all of us most of the time. It is often a way of expressing a fresh piece of the truth that institutional arteriosclerosis prevents us from understanding. The institution becomes defensive if pushed beyond where its current leaders think it ought to be. Those leaders move slowly out of their own anxiety and insecurity as they become preoccupied with the church's survival, instead of her mission. Yet God calls us to "love and forgiveness" as the basic purpose for our existence. Arno Borst adds that "the unprejudiced observer will rely on the statement of

Carl Jung, that understanding is difficult, but condemnation is easy."

My presentment plunged us into this matrix of ideas about heresy. After the House of Bishops meeting in Kanuga, we understood the fact that a political agenda was hidden under the charges made against me, but we decided to focus on dealing with the charges instead of the political agenda. From the day I received the charges in February 1995, I had ninety days to give my response, which meant I should have my response in the Presiding Bishop's hands by May twelfth.

The charges stated that my actions constituted a teaching that was contrary to the teaching of the Episcopal Church and that by doing so, I had violated my ordination vows. My defense, carefully reasoned and worded by my team of chancellors and assisted by some clergy who volunteered their services, said clearly that I had not done either of those things but that I had ordained a gay man who had a same-sex companion. The document was written by Michael Rehill of Newark and was refined during regular conferences by telephone and in person with many other advisers. My position was clear. I had ordained Barry Stopfel to the diaconate. I knew he had a lifelong same-sex partner. They were and are in love with each other. I also made it clear that Jack Spong had asked me to ordain Barry. He had not ordered me to do so. I had voluntarily done the ordination. In my own heart, I was certain I had done nothing wrong. I felt better about the ordination than I did about many of the persons I had ordained in my seventeen years as a diocesan bishop. The task of the lawyers was to cast my personal conviction in the legal framework that made it an adequate response and defense to the charges that had been made by my accusers. When the document was finished, Michael Rehill personally handed it to the Presiding Bishop on May 12, 1995. Michael went out of his way to take a whole morning of his time traveling from his law office in New Jersey to the Presiding Bishop's office in the Episcopal Center at 815 Second Avenue in New York City. The document was not only well worded and well reasoned; it was nicely printed. We all thought it should be in a form that was attractive and easy to read. We were conscious of the fact that it was a historic document and that handing it to the Presiding Bishop was a historic moment in the life of the Episcopal Church in the United States. It then became Ed Browning's responsibility to circulate the charges made against me by the ten presenters and my response as it had been framed by my defense team.

As soon as that letter was sent, people began to speculate: "There can't possibly be enough votes for a trial. How many votes do you think there will be?" The Presiding Bishop did a typically wise thing. He told his staff they were to release no figures on the vote count at any given moment. After the deadline, everyone would be told. I was pleased when I was told that. Yet there was tremendous pressure in the whole church to have some forecast of the outcome. Gays and lesbians had a profound interest in knowing whether or not there would be a trial. So did the members of the Episcopal Synod of America and Episcopalians United. Every Bishop, no matter how he or she voted, was constantly being asked by his or her constituents what was happening. The print and electronic media had began to show more than a passing interest, especially since the prior year had seen the treasurer of the Episcopal Church accused of stealing more than $2 million, and the bishop of the largest Episcopal diocese (Massachusetts) committing suicide. A retired bishop, living in the hills of New Hampshire with his wife and his golden retriever, being tried for heresy? In the twentieth century? In the United States? It was incredulous enough to be news.

That incredulity began its slow wave across the United States. Gus Niebuhr, grandson of one of my seminary professors and a reporter for the *New York Times*, called in early August and asked if he and a photographer could travel to New Hampshire to interview me. I was impressed that a Niebuhr was to visit our house. Nancy was impressed that the *New York Times* was coming. In either case, it was clear that a lot of attention was being given to this strange case.

On August fifteenth, my attorney and I awaited the vote tally, but it did not come. It seemed that the Presiding Bishop's chancellor was off on an island that was beset by storms and could not get to the mainland. It was necessary for him to examine all the votes to make sure they were in order. He did that eventually, and by August eighteenth, after my attorney expressed my insistence and his that we had a right to know what the results were, we were told that the seventy-six votes to have a trial had been mailed back, exactly the required number.

In order to be responsible about his job as my attorney, Michael Rehill went from his office in New Jersey to the Presiding Bishop's office in New York City and spent a part of one day examining the consents of the bishops. During that process, he made some fascinating discoveries. Sometime in middle or late July, the number of consents leveled off to fifty-five. Then suddenly, as the date of August fifteenth drew closer, there was a flurry of activity. It looked to me as if the number fifty-five had been discovered by my accusers. I have been told since then, by friends in the House of Bishops, that they had been called late in the time frame and had had their arms twisted to send in their consents. Some of them were opposed to my action of ordaining Barry, but they also disagreed with the idea of heresy charges. Jack Gilliam, the former Bishop of Montana, called me from Hawaii to say,

"When you did that ordination, I could have kicked you in the butt for doing it. But this trial is no way to settle the issue!" Some of them knew me well enough to know that I simply was not the kind of person to do something heretical. There obviously had been a lot of conversation by telephone or in person, some of it creating the extra twenty-one votes that finally came in.

Michael discovered some odd responses. One form had a note to the Presiding Bishop on it saying, "Ed, you're doing a good job," with a vote for a trial (Ed Browning was against the idea of a trial). Another form had a note saying, "I wasn't going to vote for the trial, but in view of the recent ordination in Washington, D.C., I've decided to vote for a trial!" (There had been an ordination of a gay person in Washington, D.C., just before he sent his vote in. What that had to do with the charges against me was a mystery, unless my trial was a political way for him to respond to the ordination.) Another bishop was unable to fill out the form himself because of Alzheimer's disease. His son had his power of attorney. So he filled out the form for his father. And he said, in effect, "Have a trial." That astounded me. The bishop, Richard Emrich, former Bishop of Michigan, was a traditionally liberal bishop in a traditionally liberal diocese. I personally would not have expected him to have voted for a trial. I have since been told, by people who knew him well, that his liberality did not extend to matters of homosexuality and the ordination of noncelibate gays and lesbians. The form, voting for a trial, was not filled out properly. According to my attorney, it was sent back by the Presiding Bishop's chancellor, David Beers, with instructions about how to do it, and it was returned after the deadline date, but it was permitted in the count.

There is no provision in the Constitution and Canons

for someone to cast a vote for a bishop about a matter as serious as this by power of attorney. Perhaps there should be, but there isn't. We did not have adequate explanation for accepting this highly irregular vote, even though it was late. But my attorney and his advisers decided against going through all kinds of detailed challenges and, instead, to stick to the main point: I had not done anything wrong.

The news that the trial process would go forward came to me in the middle of the afternoon of August eighteenth. Nancy, who works for Monadnock Family Services in Cheshire County, was at a staff picnic. I had to buzz her beeper in order to get her to call me. I wanted to tell her myself what was happening, instead of having her hear it on the car radio on the way home. I would have preferred being with her when she got the news. But it would have taken me forty-five minutes to get to the picnic site, and by that time, the radio might have carried the news and she might have heard it.

I did not know when I called her, but discovered when she got home, that the picnic was a particularly trying time for her. She is a pacifist by conviction. The picnic she was attending was a required activity for all staff, and the activity planned was a "war game" involving water pistols. The staff got carried away, and the "play" became somewhat hostile. Already concerned for me, she found herself "attacked" on more than one front.

No matter how serene and calm your nature is, it is a rude shock to learn that your peers have decided to try you when no canon has been violated, especially when there have been others among the bishops—some of them my presenters—who have clearly violated the canons of the church over the ordination of women. The charity of the House of Bishops forbore their offenses. It is an even ruder shock to one's spouse to discover that the person she loves and supports wholeheartedly is going to have to go through a trial because of having done what was the right thing.

In spite of the assurances of hundreds of people that a trial would not occur, enough bishops voted for it to make it necessary to go ahead with the process. Perhaps my supporters forgot the change in the number of votes necessary, passed at the convention in Phoenix. For surely that made all the difference. It was very difficult for my accusers to muster seventy-six votes. It would have been impossible to get two hundred. It took us several days to absorb these facts. Nancy, in particular, was blindsided, never having been exposed to the possibility of evil within the church. To discover it writ large in the House of Bishops was a horrible shock.

On September eighth, less than a month after we learned we were going to be faced with a trial process, Nancy received a thoughtful letter from Patti Browning, wife of the Presiding Bishop. It said, "Just a note to let you know that you are surely on my mind and in my prayers during these difficult days. From my own experience, I really believe it is much harder to deal with the pain inflicted on someone we love, such as spouse or children, than it is to deal with our own pain and disappointments. I hope you are feeling the prayers and support of many, including mine. All best to you."

Nancy says that letter marked a turning point for her. She recognized that the strength she was feeling was due directly to a tremendous wave of support coming our way in the prayers of thousands of persons throughout the world. It became clear to both of us that we were being supported, and that we had a privilege rare in human experience. We were able to bear witness to what we believe the basic meaning of the Christian Gospel is: unconditional love. Yet the presentment also meant that our lives would be subject to intrusions of all kinds, the kind of intrusions we had already been dealing with for more than half a year.

Our free time would be consumed by dealing with the case. Our phone would be in constant use. One day, while we were out having lunch, we received twelve calls on the answering machine in fifty minutes. We often had to go out to eat so we could disappear into the anonymity of a local restaurant and avoid the telephone. That was to be the story of our lives for the next nine months.

Our families were constantly dealing with people asking them about us and about the progress of the case. Nancy, already employed full-time in her profession, became, along with me, an office manager in our home as we sought to handle carefully whatever came our way. The print and electronic media called throughout the process. James Solheim, the Presiding Bishop's staff person for communication, was helpful in a general way in dealing with the media and was personally very supportive and encouraging.

THE ECCLESIASTICAL COURT for the Trial of a Bishop is composed of nine bishops. Three are elected each time a General Convention meets. Usually, when a bishop is asked to run for election to this court, the request is something like this: The chair of the nominating committee says, "We would like to place your name in nomination for the Court for the Trial of a Bishop. We don't plan to place any more than the necessary names in nomination. The court never has anything to do. The only time in our history when there was a trial was in 1923. Are you willing to have us place your name in nomination?" The bishop being asked will often chuckle about the whole idea—a court that never works, an uncontested election, a church that is not litigious—and say, "Sure, go ahead," not expecting to hear any more about it until his nine-year term is up and the Presiding Bishop writes him a letter thanking him for serving.

The nine people who were elected under those conditions, and who discovered they were to preside over the second trial of a bishop in the history of the Episcopal Church are as follows: To serve until 2003—the Rt. Rev. Andrew Fairfield, Bishop of North Dakota; the Rt. Rev. Douglas Theuner, Bishop of New Hampshire; the Rt. Rev. Robert Johnson, Bishop of North Carolina. To serve until 2000— the Rt. Rev. Arthur Walmsley, retired Bishop of Connecticut; the Rt. Rev. Roger White, Bishop of Milwaukee; the Rt. Rev. Edward Jones, Bishop of Indianapolis. To serve until 1997—the Rt. Rev. Donis D. Patterson, retired Bishop of Dallas; the Rt. Rev. Frederick Borsch, Bishop of Los Angeles; the Rt. Rev. Cabell Tennis, Bishop of Delaware. The senior bishop in point of service was the Rt. Rev. Edward Jones of Indianapolis. He became the president of the court.

The canons of the church call for the trial of a bishop to be held in the diocese in which he is serving or in the diocese in which he is residing. While I had been Bishop of Iowa for seventeen years, I was now retired and living in New Hampshire. I live at least an hour and a half from a major airport. The Standing Committee of the Diocese of New Hampshire had already gone on record with the Presiding Bishop, saying they did not want to be host to the trial. The court needed to decide where and when the first session of the court would be held.

The members of the court, all of whom I had known in some way or other during my life of service in the church, had to distance themselves from me completely. Access to them came solely through my attorney. Once you get involved in a trial process either in the church or in the secular world, it, by its very nature, becomes divisive and alienating. While the court tried to be thoughtful about my travel and the costs accompanying it, any opinion I had had to be expressed through my attorney.

The first suggestion that came from the court was that we meet in Chicago at St. James Cathedral. As a midwestern bishop, I had served as a trustee of Seabury-Western Seminary in Evanston, a city north of Chicago, so the airport and the environs of one of America's largest cities were familiar to me. Nancy and I made reservations in a hotel near the cathedral. But we acted too fast. Both my attorney, Michael Rehill, and the attorney for the other side, Hugo Blankingship, petitioned the court for a change of location. My attorney and I pressed for the Diocese of Newark or the Episcopal Center, 815 Second Avenue, New York City. Our reason for seeking either of those two places was simply that a number of people from the dioceses of Newark and New York wanted to attend the proceedings and observe them. Either place was a reasonable travel distance for me, much more reasonable than Chicago. The court made its decision. We were to meet at Christ Church Cathedral in Hartford, Connecticut, on December eighth at 9:00 a.m. A Eucharist would precede the meeting.

Because the court had made its decision so late, Nancy and I found ourselves with an intense travel schedule. We had planned to take part in a diocesan gathering in the Diocese of Newark the night before, at St. Peter's, Morristown. That gathering was to be preceded by supper at the bishop's house with Jack and Christine Spong and Ed and Patti Browning. Ed was to be the preacher. While the choice of Hartford was made partly to be convenient for me, our commitments made the travel hectic. We drove for five hours on December 7, 1995, to get to the Spongs' in time for supper. We attended the gathering in Morristown largely to symbolize the kind of inclusivity the people of that diocese had spent years working toward, and then drove partway to Hartford (two hours of driving) and spent the night in a motel. We left the motel on December eighth, early enough to drive to Hartford and be there by nine o'clock. But traffic was heavy and we arrived almost as the clock struck nine. The dean of the cathedral was waiting for us and welcomed us warmly.

In his remarks, there was no question of his support for us as the court procedures began. I had attended seminary in New Haven, Connecticut, and one of my closest friends was the dean of the cathedral while I was in seminary—the man I had the bull session with about heresy. I had been to the cathedral before and had been welcomed warmly. It was pleasant, after all those years, to sense the same kind of welcome and the same degree of warmth, even though lots of other things had changed since 1951.

I sat down in the seat reserved for me next to my attorney. Ted Jones, the president of the court, told me that everyone had had a chance to introduce themselves before I got there, and he asked if I would introduce myself to complete the task. I did, saying, "I'm Walter Righter, the heretic." The silence in the room was immense, almost palpable!

We proceeded now to the arguments. My antagonists asked that some of the members of the court be removed, because, among other reasons, they had been involved in ordaining gay or lesbian persons living in same-sex relationships and thus were allegedly prejudiced about the case. My attorney and his associates at first thought they would seek the removal of other members of the court who would be prejudiced on the other side of things, but they decided to accept the court and not seek the removal of any of the judges. They stuck to the central issue: I had done nothing wrong.

A further complication arose. The brief for my accusers had been prepared by the Rt. Rev. William Wantland,

Bishop of Eau Claire, Wisconsin. Bill Wantland had been a lawyer before he was ordained. The brief was described by Stephen Jecko, Bishop of Florida, in one of his diocesan publications as "superb." My brief was terse and to the point. It was historically accurate and theologically sound; a markedly distinguished professional document. But before we got to Hartford, we began to hear that my accusers wanted to make some additional arguments besides those they had in their brief. It was obvious to me, at least, that what they had provided was not "superb," that they knew it, and that they wanted space to rectify it. My attorney objected. The additional arguments that my accusers put forth warped the whole case and tried to move it into another conceptual field.

The presenters, by this time represented not only by Bill Wantland but also by Hugo Blankingship, an attorney from the Diocese of Virginia, attempted to present the additional argument. At that first pretrial hearing, Wantland was lead attorney for the presenters. Michael objected to Bill pleading the case, since he was the author and one of the signers of the presentment. Wantland persisted in interrupting my attorney as he was pursuing his argument. Even though he was a bishop and a priest, he seemed to take pleasure in acting as an attorney. If it had not been for the fact that I was the object of the charges, I could have appreciated the intense drama of it all. Blankingship did some of the pleading, as well. We broke for lunch. The early afternoon brought some more sparring until 3:00 p.m., when the court announced that it wanted to talk with the accusers and the accused and their attorneys in private and dismissed everyone else. It also announced that the decision had been made not to disqualify anyone from sitting on the court.

A final announcement, made before everyone was asked to leave, was that the Bishop of Connecticut, Clarence

Coleridge, had asked us not to return to Hartford for any more trial proceedings. It seems Clarence had had to deal with more media attention than he wanted, and as a result of that, he had had to handle an enormous number of telephone calls about the case. He said he did not have the time in his schedule to handle that kind of work and that we would have to leave. The dean of the cathedral circulated a paper telling us he understood the necessity for the bishop to make the decision he was making, but he wanted us to know we were, from the cathedral's point of view, still very welcome.

The Bishop of Delaware, Cabell Tennis, who was also a member of the court, offered an invitation to come to his diocese the next time we met, and it was accepted. As we reconvened in a kind of executive session, there seemed to be a sifting out of some arguments. Members of the court asked both sides some questions they had been thinking about. Sally Johnson, the chancellor of the Diocese of Minnesota, and formally appointed the lay assessor (an adviser to the court on legal matters, but not theological matters), raised a question that seemed to focus what was happening. She said, "Would both sides agree that if this is about doctrine, we should proceed; if it is not, the case ends?" Both sides agreed to that. Both sides were to focus on that the next time we met. My accusers had tried to slide into disciplinary matters, instead of sticking to doctrinal ones. They additionally had tried to convert into doctrine a number of issues and decisions that were not ever conceived to be doctrinal. They would continue to try to do so, in order to salvage their case. With that agreement, the day's proceedings ended.

It had been an exhausting day for everyone, especially for Nancy and me, but I felt satisfied that an appropriate step had been taken. We were far from finished, but to focus the argument the next time on whether or not this whole case was about doctrine seemed, to me, a step forward. We were now to watch some convoluted efforts to change the whole accusation from one of doctrinal violation to disciplinary violation, and additional efforts to make the doctrinal umbrella large enough to allow my accusers to change the course of their accusation.

The basic question still echoed throughout all the proceedings: What kind of church is the Episcopal Church? Inclusive? Exclusive? Some arbitrary combination of both—depending upon the personal opinion of the bishop of each diocese? Other questions also arose. What place does Scripture have in the Episcopal Church? Is it to be interpreted literally? Is Scripture to be used as a means of judging others? Is it to be interpreted by the church carefully asking always, "What do these words mean?" What place tradition? What is it that produces tradition? And, coincidentally, what produces doctrine? Does a single General Convention motion, arrived at by hours of argument in committee and finally put into compromise language, create both tradition and doctrine? What place reason? Do people understand what the Caroline divines meant by that word? Do they know that reason served the social contract? (In correspondence with one of my fellow bishops during these proceedings, he told me he did not believe in any such thing as a social contract!) What is the church's role in shaping the social contract? Do our ordained leaders understand how profound their role is in times of massive change in the social contract?

These questions form part of the constellation of ideas that were circling around this attempt to get a clear statement about sexuality by means of a trial. Nancy and I left the court, and the cathedral where it had met, exhausted emotionally and spiritually. We ate supper together in a nearby restaurant. By this time, we had become adept at debriefing each other, comparing impressions and opinions. She left Hartford to drive to Long Island for a visit with her daughter, Kathy, and I left for an hour-and-a-half drive to New Hampshire. As we drove, we both found ourselves exhausted physically but glad to have this preliminary phase of things over.

I was deeply disappointed in the Bishop of Connecticut, but I was gratified by the tedious work that the members of the court seemed to be willing to do. I was pleased with the incisive questioning of Sally Johnson, the lay assessor. I was not surprised by the strength of the anger that was in me, but I was amazed that I couldn't reduce the strength of that anger. Not content with attempting to manipulate me, my accusers were trying to bully and manipulate the court by changing their argument in midstream.

If the court had allowed the change in argument, it would have meant mass confusion. The net effect would have been something like this. It would have meant that my attorney and his coworkers would have had to produce a new brief, entirely different from the one that they had meticulously prepared. Then the Presiding Bishop would have had to circulate both briefs again to every member of the House of Bishops, asking them if they thought those briefs called for a trial, and then we would have had a long waiting period, and some more arm-twisting to get seventy-six votes. It would have been the only fair and clear way to deal with a complete change of argument.

The fact that my presenters were trying to make the change without paying that kind of price was symbolic of their determination to "win" at any cost. It was entirely consistent with their behavior in bringing the accusations in the first place. Unable to get the General Convention to do what they wanted, they sought to get around our constitutional process indirectly. To tie up the whole Episcopal Church, causing enormous amounts of time, energy, and money to be spent on such a fruitless, limited, and unethical exercise, made me see red. As I drove home through the rain alone, I boiled and cogitated. It kept me awake after a tiring day.

CHAPTER 7

Wilmington

WHILE THE IMPENDING TRIAL was a terrible intrusion in our lives, there were some rewarding moments, as well. The media was continuously fascinated by the idea of a heresy trial in the twentieth century. Via the telephone, E-mail, or "snail mail," we were hearing from people from all over the world, including such exotic and faraway places as Tunisia and Moscow. Roman Catholic bishops, Jewish rabbis, Unitarian/Universalist ministers and members of their churches, and United Church of Christ clergy wrote with offers of support and encouragement. One clergy family wrote a letter of support, accompanied by a check for five hundred dollars, which represented what they would have spent for Christmas presents for one another. They had decided to forgo their presents in order to help out with my trial. Desmond Tutu, Archbishop of South Africa, stated clearly his convictions about homosexuality, and he sent a check for one hundred dollars to the Righter Defense Fund. Interestingly, I had lots of very supportive mail from the people of the dioceses whose bishops had signed the presentment.

In all, Nancy and I received over three thousand letters and as many telephone calls and E-mail notes. Only four of them were negative. One of the four was from a cousin of mine in Canada, and one was from a lady in a nearby town who thought I should attend a Bible class that she would lead.

A whole sea change in attitudes had occurred in the years between Jack Spong's ordination of Robert Williams in 1989 and the filing of the accusation against me in 1995. Following the ordination of Robert Williams, Jack Spong received something like seventy-five letters a day, 80 percent of which was orchestrated "hate" mail. Groups wanted their members to harass him. Even bishops wanted to harass him. One bishop told him he would do everything he could for the rest of his life to have Jack tried for what he had done. Another told him he would harass him for the rest of his life. Nancy and I did not experience that kind of mail or that degree of intolerance.

It is still true that the subject of homosexuality and marriage between same-sex partners touches deep concerns in many, and raises anger and hostility in others. We have to stay engaged in conversation about that. The church needs to be clear about its mission and ministry to gay and lesbian people. Some clarity is appearing randomly among the major denominations in the United States, and in other parts of the world, as well. Other, more conscious efforts to address the needs of gays and lesbians in the church include the able and unusual ministry of a priest named David Norgard. Elected as director of Oasis after Robert Williams's resignation, that ministry began to penetrate the life of the entire diocese of Newark and beyond. The Rev. Elizabeth Kaeton is now the priest in charge of that ministry and David has been called to be rector of a parish in San Francisco.

George Hunt, the retired Bishop of Rhode Island, wrote me a letter when I was presented for trial. He had retired, but he was serving as interim bishop in Hawaii. His letter pointed out that he wished he could go to trial for me, especially since he had ordained more gay and lesbian people than Jack Spong and I combined. George had been consistently supportive of me. In 1991, at Phoenix, Arizona, during a meeting of the General Convention, when the censure resolution came before the House. George Hunt was one of the first bishops to stand up and say, "If we're going to have a resolution of censure, add my name to the list of those to be censured, because I've done it, too." He is indicative of a small group of bishops who were being vocal at that convention about their support. Since that time, their number has grown.

All over the country, chapters of Integrity have formed in the years since its founding in 1974. They were incensed by the horrible treatment Jack Spong received in 1989. PFLAG (Parents and Friends of Lesbians and Gays) formed chapters, offering support to families and friends of gay and lesbian persons. They, too, became sharply aroused by the news of my proposed trial.

In the weeks prior to Wilmington, Nancy and I became aware not only of the increasing visibility of the gay community but of real changes in many people's attitudes toward inclusion, wholeness, the valuing of each human being's spiritual life. Perhaps the Vietnam War affected the body politic in ways we are still discovering, offering the value of human life a fresh charter. Certainly the churches in many denominations were designating themselves "welcoming congregations," and almost every mainline denomination has had to wrestle at its national legislative sessions with resolutions seeking more inclusiveness.

We also had some very specific examples to encourage

us. Barry Stopfel is a fine priest and has become an effective rector in the parish of St. George's, Maplewood, New Jersey. Supporting him gave us a chance to be quite clear about the theology we were espousing and the human values springing from that theology. Pointing to him as a clear example of what we were talking about and pointing to Will and their relationship with each other gave us both great pleasure and satisfaction. Their friendship is one of the greatest gifts we received in the midst of what was happening. The parish of St. George's is a delight to contemplate, as well. It has grown by 30 percent since Barry became its rector. The growth, while derived in part from the gay and lesbian community, is due mainly to young couples with small children who want an inclusive experience for themselves and their children. While I was writing this narrative in January 1997, Barry called to see how Nancy and I were faring. I asked him what kind of Christmas he and Will had had, and a part of his reply included the fact that St. George's Christmas offering was twenty-six thousand dollars.

So for each of the intrusions Nancy and I suffered, we had counterevidence, love, and support buoying us up. Seldom are people given the opportunity to bear witness clearly to the faith they hold. Even less frequently does a couple have the opportunity we have had to bear that witness in such a public way and over such a long period of time.

One of my favorite prayers in the 1979 prayer book is the "Thanksgiving for the Mission of the Church" (p. 838):

Almighty God, you sent your Son Jesus Christ to reconcile the world to yourself: We praise and bless you for those whom you have sent in the power of the Spirit to preach the Gospel to all nations. We thank you that in all parts of the earth a commu-

nity of love has been gathered together by their prayers and labor.

We felt the power of that community of love. We also felt stimulated and pleased by the work which both print and electronic media did in reporting the story of what was happening. They were fair and thorough 99 percent of the time. One reporter wrote us a note saying that this story and our approach to it made her work doing "picky stuff" worthwhile. A technician for the ABC television network sent me an E-mail note the evening of the day he worked with us on a broadcast, telling me that working with us was an experience in which he sensed spirituality at work. Over and over, Nancy and I were impressed with the quality of people who were doing the reporting as well as with their technical expertise. We have no media horror stories to report.

My accusers were not as thoughtful as the media. James Stanton, the Bishop of Dallas, sent a copy of the presentment to all of the clergy in that diocese. It should not have been sent out to anyone in bulk until it could be accompanied by my defense brief, yet at the time of Stanton's mailing, my brief had not been written. Both the charges and the defense are to be circulated to all bishops of the church so they can make a decision about whether or not there should be a trial. I did not think it fair for the clergy of a whole diocese to be given only one side of the story.

It backfired in several ways. I received a telephone call from one of the laymen in that diocese, who said, "I'm so mad at the bishop here, I want to give one thousand dollars to your defense fund!" I am told by others in that diocese that the rectors of the largest parishes gathered at a meeting with the bishop and made it quite clear that they considered Jim Stanton's action in signing the presentment a mistake. Ben

Benitez, the Bishop of Texas when the presentment was made, but the retired bishop less than a week afterward, wrote a long article for one of the periodicals in the Episcopal communication pipeline justifying the presentment. I wrote him immediately, suggesting clearly that I thought we were going to have a trial to test the charges being made and saying I did not think it was helpful to have him plead the case in a church periodical before anyone had seen my defense. He responded by saying he thought my speech at the Kanuga House of Bishops' meeting had been pleading my case (which it was not) and that therefore he was justified in arguing it in a magazine article.

As the process unfolded, it became more and more clear that heresy was not the issue for my accusers and their adherents. Louie Crew is also a member of the Human Affairs Commission of the General Convention of the Episcopal Church. Ed Salmon, Bishop of South Carolina and chair of the commission, made a remark in Louie's presence, showing how far afield his interpretation of the actions of my accusers were. He said, to Louie and to other members of the commission as they gathered for a meeting, "This case is not about sexuality; it's about order and discipline." Louie, who has a quick and very perceptive mind, responded by saying, "Bishop, do you mean that all the members of the gay and lesbian community are being scapegoated?" Ed Salmon didn't even take time to think. He said, "Yes!"

Before we went to Wilmington to continue the trial process, St. James Church, Keene, New Hampshire, our parish church, performed a very thoughtful act. The interim rector, Murdoch Smith, although somewhat uncomfortable with the whole question of how the church should treat its gay and lesbian members, was also committed to inclusivity as a church practice. He had been completely supportive of Nancy and me. For a time, I was listed among the clergy of the parish on the weekly bulletin. When it became public that I was being charged with heresy, one of the members of St. James Church called on Murdoch to demand he strike my name from the list of clergy. If that did not happen, he said, he would have to find another place to worship. Murdoch politely asked him, "How can I help you find that place?" That kind of personal support was unwavering. It went beyond that, however. The parish held a service on the Saturday afternoon before we went to the hearing in Wilmington. It was an ecumenical event as well as a parish event. People from neighboring communities and a variety of faith communities were invited and came, as well as Nancy's coworkers and even her hairdresser; Episcopalians from the Church of the Good Shepherd, Nashua, New Hampshire, where I had been rector for seventeen years before becoming bishop; Episcopalians from Proctorsville, Springfield, and Bellows Falls, Vermont; UCC members from Jaffrey, Keene, and Alstead, New Hampshire; Methodists from Surrey, Keene, and Alstead; one of my Des Moines clergy now living in Vermont, as well as his wife; and a sizable number of all age groups from St. James Church itself.

Judy Putnam, vestry person and friend at St. James, had T-shirts made with our names on them and this message: "You are surrounded by our love and prayers." Everyone present was given an opportunity to sign the T-shirts. Their names symbolized, for us, our sense of being surrounded. Among the many signers were my son, Richard, and his wife, Shirley; the rector, Murdoch Smith, and his wife, Linda; and a friend, Terry Warren, who also signed for her cat Tabitha. Nancy and I took to Wilmington a real sense of a gathered community of faith supporting us through those days with love and prayers.

Since Philadelphia is the nearest city with a major airport to Wilmington, Delaware, we flew there and were to be met by Stephen Snider. He had agreed to give us ground transportation to the hotel in Wilmington where the key people in the trial were staying. As we deplaned and started our walk to the luggage carousel, we were met by a reporter for CNN who wanted to do an interview before we left the airport. She had arranged for a private room for the interview. The idea of someone being tried for heresy was hot news! As we walked toward the private room, I watched for Steve. He has a mischievous side, which usually surfaces unexpectedly. It did that day. As we walked, Nancy and I spotted a huge hand-lettered sign. Unlike a lot of signs held up by people who are meeting other people, it did not have my name written on it. It said TROUBLEMAKER! Behind the sign was a smiling Stephen Snider. All of us had a good laugh. After that, the interview was done in a very relaxed way.

Driving to Wilmington from the Philadelphia airport was a nostalgic experience for me. Many of my forebears had lived in Delaware, just over the line from Pennsylvania. A great-aunt and great-uncle once had a farm on some of the land we were driving through, overlooking the Delaware River. During summer visits, it used to be great fun to sit in their fields and watch boats on the river.

Suddenly, we were in Wilmington and looking for the hotel. The people of the Diocese of Delaware, under Cabby Tennis's leadership, were a most hospitable bunch. The Suffragan Bishop of the Diocese of Newark, Jack McKelvey, had grown up in Wilmington. He had been an acolyte at the cathedral and a Boy Scout. He came for the trial session and voluntarily acted as chaplain for Nancy and me. With Jack's help, three events had been arranged by three clergy who were new to the Diocese of Delaware. They all had a sensitivity about coming to a new place and not knowing a soul, so they arranged events to help us feel at home. As soon as we got to Wilmington, there were media people there who wanted to interview us again. A woman from the Baltimore paper, who had talked with me at great length on the phone at home, wanted to meet us. One of the major TV networks wanted an interview for the evening news. Nancy and I had eaten no lunch and it was almost 2:30 p.m. We went into the hotel dining room with Steve Snider to have a quick meal.

Seated near us were the editor of *Episcopal Life*, Jerry Hames, and a staff writer, Nan Cobbey. As I got my things together to go up to the room, Nancy and Steve were stopped by Jerry and Nan. Jerry Hames suggested to her not only that I had been singled out as a target for the presentment but that many people thought this was a way of denying Jack Spong the national opportunity to speak to the issue. "Get" Jack Spong but deny him the spotlight or opportunity for response.

Suddenly, it was time to go to the first event, an evening worship service at Trinity Church, Wilmington, whose rector is Anne Bonnyman-Lippincott. This was a place to pray and ask God for support and guidance. The celebrant at the Eucharist was Cynthia Black, a superb priest I had met during my time in the Diocese of Newark. She had moved from being the assistant in Essex Fells, New Jersey, to being rector of the cathedral congregation in Kalamazoo, Michigan. At that point, she was the president of the national Episcopal Women's Caucus, whose members were staunch supporters of me during this trial period.

The arrangements Jack McKelvey made were thorough and complete. We were picked up by someone from the Diocese of Delaware and driven directly to the church. As we got out of the car, I was stunned by bright lights, microphones, and questions being shouted at me by what seemed like a hundred people from the media. They were all doing their job and seeking a quick sound bite they could use for their evening news program. When asked what my feelings were about the next day, all I could think of to say was, "I came to worship. I would like to do that." And we did. The media people backed off, somewhat reluctantly.

As we waited in the church for the service to begin, we realized we were surrounded by the Communion of Saints. The hymns were sung lustily (as John Wesley recommended during his lifetime), the sermon preached by Jack McKelvey was pointedly appropriate, Cynthia celebrated beautifully, and we gradually found our way out of the church and to the parking lot, where we were to meet our ride and be taken back to the hotel. I met an old friend for the first time in a number of years—Charlie Price, retired professor of theology at Virginia Theological Seminary, who was there doing an article for the Episcopal News Service. I also made a number of new friends.

The media people, who had waited patiently for the church service to end, now sought out comments from Nancy and me about our hopes and expectations for the next day and our feelings about the whole process. It was easy for both of us to say we hoped and expected that our case would be pleaded brilliantly the next day. It was harder for us to describe our feelings during the past year. We had both been on an emotional roller coaster, going from anger to despair to confidence, ending up feeling called by God to proclaim the Gospel message of unconditional love and our own baptismal promise to respect the dignity of every living person.

By this time we were feeling confident that we were doing what was *right*. But it was important for people to understand that we had also experienced the roller-coaster effect, and the pain of despair and anger. The ten fellow bishops who had accused me needed to be kept continuously aware of the way their manipulative actions affected people throughout the church, and Nancy and I were exhibit number one. So we tried to bear that witness. Our car and driver arrived to take us back to the hotel.

We had not yet eaten supper, but we had another stop to make before doing that. Late in the afternoon, people from Ted Koppel's *Nightline* called and asked us to be on the show. The entire half hour was to be devoted to the Episcopal Church and its heresy trial. A crisis was brewing in the relations between the United States and Cuba, but we learned from other media people that the proceedings in Wilmington were being given precedence over that story.

Almost as soon as we landed at the hotel, a car arrived to pick us up and take us to the taping for *Nightline*. We were to record the show in Wilmington at 9:30 p.m. and it would be aired later that evening. We arrived early for the taping, but they were having technical difficulties. There was obvious tension among the crew in Wilmington, and also between the Wilmington people and the Washington, D.C., crew as they tried to get the problems straightened out. One technician, who was hooking up my microphone and arranging my seating, asked me if I had any questions. I answered, "Yes. Are there going to be any trick questions?" He shrugged his shoulders and said nothing, but a few minutes later Ted Koppel came on the audio and said, "Bishop, how are you doing?" I told him I was fine and that I hoped we could get the taping done soon, since neither Nancy nor I had eaten dinner. He allowed as to how he would like that to happen soon, as well. Then he made this comment: "Bishop, if there is any pain involved in this tonight, it won't be inflicted by us!" In the midst of all the technical problems they were experiencing, the technician had taken time to tell the production people about my anxiety about trick questions, and Ted Koppel had taken the time to reassure me even as he was trying to get the taping started. One of the fine new prayers in our 1979 prayer book is one entitled "For Those Who Influence Public Opinion." Each time I read it, I think of all those media people who spent so much time on this strange heresy case, and of the fine work they did.

We finally got back to our hotel at 10:30 p.m. and found the food-service section of the hotel almost ready to close. They had stopped cooking the evening meal, but they agreed to get us hamburgers. By the time we arrived at our room, we were completely exhausted. After watching *Nightline*, and feeling very good about that program, we went to bed and slept, as the saying goes, "the sleep of the dead."

The next morning there was a Eucharist at the cathedral, where Peggy Patterson, the new dean, was the preacher. The second lesson, Ephesians 2:13–22, got Nancy giggling, along with some folks from Integrity who were sitting behind us. The words were written for us. "You are no longer strangers and foreigners, but fellow citizens with the saints in the kingdom of God." And the Gospel, Luke 10:1–9 is a mission statement: "Go as lambs in the midst of wolves." Truly prophetic words.

The significance of these words had been impressed upon me in a very pragmatic way during the very beginning of my ministry. While I was in seminary, the Bishop of Pittsburgh sent me to Aliquippa each summer. The congregation of All Saints Church had had several clergymen who did not stay long and with whom they did not seem to get along. The bishop had said to them, "In view of what's happened between you and the clergy who have been here, you must wait a while before you get a full-time priest." Each Sunday, a retired priest or a lay reader took services. For weddings and funerals, the bishop's office arranged the presence of a priest. In the meantime, Sunday school, choir, altar guild, vestry, and other activities continued with local leadership. Bishop Pardue sent me there the summer after my first year in seminary (1949). I was there for three months. My wife and I lived in a tiny house owned by a nurse who was away at school for the summer. My three months constituted the longest continuous ministry the people of All Saints parish had had in almost ten years. Aliquippa was laid out on twelve hills. Each hill was called a "Plan" and each plan was for a specific group of people: Plan 6 was for the superintendents; Plan 12 was for the middle-class workers in the steel mill or the company's stores, or by-products divisions; Plan 11 was for the laborers; and so forth. The people who lived in the community were from the British Isles, Europe, and the southern part of the United States (largely black). Some of my parishioners were part of a large family whose father had come to the United States from Prague, Czechoslovakia, and was employed by the local bank in the early days of the history of the town. He could speak almost all European languages and became the person who helped European people transact their affairs with the bank. He did that work for almost a whole generation.

While there that first summer, I realized why Roman Catholic clergy were from so many different nations, and why Roman Catholic parishes often had national designations next to their names. The clergy were the people who helped new immigrants understand and cope with the system called the United States of America. The Episcopal Church is often thought of as the English church, particularly in a community like Aliquippa where everyone was so conscious of national origins. But All Saints Church was not "the English church." People of many nationalities were involved in the worship and activities of the parish. They had come during their lifetimes from many different denominations of the Christian world into the Episcopal Church. My first Sunday among them, I somehow had to recognize all their diversity and do it in an appreciative way. I looked up the lessons for the day, and there it was, this marvelous text that Peggy Patterson used the day the court hearings began: "You are no longer strangers and foreigners, but fellow citizens with the saints in the kingdom of God." That day in Wilmington, we had an opportunity to continue God's work of inclusion, begun in the presence of Jesus Christ almost two thousand years before and continued in each generation of the life of the church ever since. I had the opportunity to recall that part of my ministry that began with inclusivity at its heart. That is what the whole court case was about. I had come full cycle.

Peggy Patterson's sermon was pointedly appropriate. In part, this is what Peggy said: "Just as the most difficult, most painful part of childbirth comes just before the baby is born, in the almost-life-threatening period of transition through the narrow birth canal, so I believe God is bringing to birth through our pain a new vision for the church, which will embody the promises we have heard in the letter to the Ephesians." Powerful words. My hope was that they would prove to be true.

COURT CONVENED IMMEDIATELY following the service. The arguments began with the air cleared. In Hartford, Connecticut, in December 1995, there had been a motion made by my accusers to disqualify four of the judges of the court because they had knowingly ordained a noncelibate homosexual and because they, like me, had signed the "Statement of Koinonia" at the General Convention in Indianapolis, Indiana, in 1994. The court issued a memorandum stating, "The court polled its members and each and every judge confirmed that he is, in fact . . . impartial regarding the case at hand."

Another motion by my accusers was aimed at disqualifying lay assessor Sally Johnson, chancellor of the Diocese of Minnesota, because she was a chancellor. A canon that became effective January 1, 1996, says that chancellors may not serve as lay assessors. The court ruled that the new canon could not be applied retroactively to disqualify Ms. Johnson.

A third ruling by the court declined to allow the Rt. Rev. William Wantland, Bishop of Eau Claire, to act as counsel for my accusers, since he was one of them himself and a potential witness. He had, despite objections by my attorney, Michael Rehill, participated as counsel in the pretrial hearing in Hartford in December.

These rulings were all mild victories for my attorney. My accusers, aware of the inadequacy of their brief, had pushed in several directions to find some advantageous weak spot, and it had not worked.

The presentment against me, written by William Wantland and signed by him and nine other bishops with jurisdiction, said this in Section IX:

> A Bishop . . . of this Church shall be liable to presentment and trial for the following offenses, viz:
>
> (2) Holding and teaching publicly or privately, and advisedly, any doctrine contrary to that held by this church.
>
> (6) Any act which involved a violation of his Ordination vows.
>
> Count 1:
>
> Respondent is hereby charged with violation of Canon IV.1. 1(2) in that he is teaching publicly and advisedly that a practicing homosexual may properly be ordained to the diaconate or priesthood, and has rejected the Doctrine of

the Church that it is impermissible to ordain a practicing and or advocating homosexual. He is therefore teaching a doctrine contrary to that held by this Church.

    Count 2:

    Respondent is hereby charged with violation of Canon IV. 1.1(6) in that he ordained a practicing homosexual to the diaconate, knowing the ordinand to be a practicing homosexual, in violation of the teaching of the Church, and thus committing an act in violation of his ordination vows to "conform to the Doctrine . . . of the . . . Church," and in the face of the declaration of the House of Bishops that "no Bishop of this Church shall confer Holy Orders in violation of" the principle that "In the case of an advocating and/or practicing homosexual, ordination is inadmissible."

Note the key word in each charge: *doctrine.*

The language of my accusers, even though it was expressed in legalese, was horrible to hear. I cringed to hear my gay and lesbian friends characterized as Hugo Blankingship spoke. He used words like *pederasty, sexual violations,* and *pedophilia* to describe homosexual behavior. It is, in the words of my attorney, "irresponsible and intellectually dishonest" to accuse all homosexuals of those practices. Not only in my accusers' insistence on the literal use of Holy Scripture but also in their interpretation of their literal use of biblical writings, they showed the world a group of people who absolutely refuse to acknowledge that words always contain a deeper meaning than can be found in just the words themselves. For three hours, we were subjected to language that sought to show the Episcopal Church has a doctrine I had violated by ordaining Barry Stopfel.

It soon became clear that Blankingship was trying to interpret the sources of doctrine as broadly as possible. He said, "This case is about authority—order—marriage—family values." The judges asked questions constantly. One of the questions put to Blankingship went something like this: "If, as you say, there is a doctrine that makes ordination of practicing homosexual persons unlawful, then what is to happen to all the practicing homosexuals who are now ordained and ministering in Christ's name in the church?" Mr. Blankingship stunned me, as well as a lot of other people, with his reply. "I can't answer that. You bishops will have to deal with that and figure it out. You've gotta remember—I'm the lawyer who got stuck with this case!" Spoken in court, in front of his clients, by a lawyer who had too much on his plate.

A group of people from the Diocese of Delaware took us to Winterthur, a Du Pont mansion turned museum, for lunch. It was a decided change from the morning's proceedings and a pleasant diversion. But as soon as Michael Rehill began his defense statement in the afternoon, we were brought back to reality. He challenged the attempt of his opponent to broaden the idea of doctrine by using such words as *authority, order, marriage, family values.* Michael said what he and his advisers had said from the very beginning: "This case is about whether there is a doctrine in the Episcopal Church prohibiting this ordination." This was a clear and concise argument. As Blankingship proceeded to rebuttal, he revealed his fears when he said we would stand alone if we permitted ordination of noncelibate homosexuals. Michael, in his rebuttal, dealt carefully and in a straightforward way with the questions coming from the most conservative bishop on the court to the most liberal. He cited the absence of any word from Jesus about homosexuality, and he said the summary of the law "love your neighbor as yourself" was Jesus' way of teaching us about relationships and about love and compassion.

As the argument ended and prayers of dismissal were said, I thought again of being engaged in a transforming moment in church history. Traditions do not end or change easily, and revelation is such a startling event; we were engaged that day in trying to understand both changing traditions and the presence of continuing revelation in our lives as God affects them. And as each occurs, the world is involved in a constant process of transforming itself. Sexuality, male dominance, the basic meaning of the Christian faith—all were at stake in this case and in that day's arguments. We then awaited the court's response, certain that they would need some time to discuss what their conclusions would be.

The implications of the statements by Bishop Wantland on behalf of the ten presenters were then, and still are, enormous. They attempted to hold hostage approximately 20 million people in the United States alone—gays, lesbians, and their families and friends. The appeal to tradition is an old argument for Christians. Peter and Paul, two of the earliest Christian leaders, had this argument: Peter said, "Tradition requires that all males be circumcised." Paul responded, "Our mission calls us to put that tradition aside in order to share God's good news in Jesus Christ with all people." Paul won that argument, and it is my hope that the same kind of mission-oriented approach will prevail as we enter the twenty-first century of Christian life and work.

When the ideas and tactics of my accusers are permitted to stand against the classic arguments of the church's past, and the continuous reaffirmation of ministry and mission throughout two thousand years, their threats appear ridiculous. The continuing decisions of the General Convention to refuse to deny ordination for homosexuals is clearly mission-oriented. If my accusers won the right to proceed to try all the bishops, each trial would take fifteen months to play itself out. Each trial would cost at least a quarter of a million dollars for the defense. The costs of the accusers are paid out of the treasury of the national church, from moneys provided by the members of the Episcopal Church all over the United States. Based upon figures available at the end of the proceedings against me, the accusers' costs would be roughly $150,000. In addition, that treasury would have to be prepared to pay lawyers' fees and travel costs for eighty-seven and a half years! More than seventy bishops would have to go to trial. The trials would not come to an end until the year 2082, in the first century of the third millennium of the Christian Era.

The same sense of righteousness that could propose what I have just outlined was quite clear as the pretrial hearings began. Having received assent from both sides at our meeting in Hartford that we would argue about whether or not this case was about doctrine, my accusers proceeded in Wilmington to try to broaden the charges that were made against me, and to seek to charge me with violations of the discipline of the church as well as the doctrine, thus showing again that their charges were not really about any "heresy" that I had committed. They had no charges grounded in sound principle; rather, they sought to bend and reshape their arguments in order to win at any price.

The court acted brilliantly when it focused our arguments on whether or not this whole case was about doctrine, as the accusers had originally proposed. By gaining assent from both sides in Hartford in December that this case was about doctrine, and then insisting that we stick to that point, the court managed to keep control where it ought to be and to limit the kind of shotgun arguments that my accusers obviously wanted to make. The pretrial arguments by my attorney, Michael Rehill, set the tone and will, I believe, be studied by canon lawyers and seminary students for some generations. The pretrial arguments of my accusers will be seen, I believe, as a desperate attempt to achieve, at any cost, what they were really seeking in the first place—an orchestrated effort to get the court to give them the power that the General Convention and the House of Bishops had refused them. It had not worked in the General Convention. It had not worked in the House of Bishops. Now they were attempting to make it happen through an ecclesiastical court. With the statement of the court, read by the seventh Bishop of Delaware, Cabell Tennis, in May of 1996, in his cathedral church of St. Andrew in Wilmington, Delaware, the tactics of my accusers failed.

The court did deliberate, and it gave us very short notice about what we have come to call "Wilmington II." On April 25, 1996, we were notified that we were expected to be in Wilmington on May fifteenth. In spite of the short notice, there was relief; at last we were to find out if there was to be a trial or not, even though it would have seemed to most observers that a trial had already taken place. But at last we were to get a definitive word; was there a doctrine I had violated? The Court's judgment was no. Was there a discipline I had violated? Again, the answer was no. No more wondering, no more doubt, about what would happen to Barry and Will and other members of the gay and lesbian community. No more pressure on Nancy and me to deal with the legalisms, while bearing our own witness. We could not, however, go out and celebrate. We could not shout, "Hosanna," or even "Hooray!" We had to sit through statements by two concurring bishops and a horrible denunciation of womanhood and all gay and lesbian people by Andrew Fairfield, Bishop of North Dakota.

Fairfield spoke sternly and did his best to disagree with the court, using the Book of Genesis and the Book of Leviticus and their proscriptions against incest, bestiality, and homosexual acts. He said the ordination of gays and lesbians who are noncelibate violates the creative purposes of God, and he expanded that argument to include the notion that a woman was incomplete in the eyes of God unless she had a man by her side. I had heard so much complicated argument all morning that I was finding it difficult to stay alert and listen. Rage renewed my energy. As Fairfield spoke, the resistance to what he was saying became almost palpable. Will, Barry's partner, said he was almost ready to walk out. Nancy told me later, "If Will had walked out, I would have followed." They were far from alone. The arrogance and the smug conceit involved in lumping gay and lesbian people in one group, calling them all immoral, and using the Bible as justification were almost too much to bear.

During the first Wilmington pretrial hearing, Cabby Tennis asked the question that pointed to the way in which doctrine grows and changes. Underlying his question was the belief that we are all participants in some form of continuing revelation from God to us. We have seen revelation at work throughout history—especially recent U.S. history, and the history of the Episcopal Church. Even as the church dragged her feet, slavery was abolished in our country. Racism today, if not abolished, is at least on the defensive. Women have achieved more than a little success in being recognized as children of God, and therefore equal to men. In the church, we have gotten to a place where ordained women are recognized, both as priests and bishops, and bring immense talent and a fresh and more complete view of God's creation. In spite of all of our disagreements, grace has constantly emerged. The pretrial process and the judgment of the court now makes it possible for us to continue to find deeper grace and fresh revelation about God and God's love and compassion and forgiveness.

On Wednesday, June 12, 1996, my accusers released a statement, written by their attorney, saying they would not appeal the decision of the court. It now was possible for the General Convention of the Episcopal Church to resume civil discourse about a variety of issues, including the major one—what kind of church we will be. The distracting and destructive nature of litigation had ended, and the church could now return to being a community of faithful persons capable of profound dialogue with one another.

CHAPTER 8

Undercurrents

The conservative who resists change is as valuable as the radical who proposes it—as perhaps much more valuable as roots are more vital than grafts. It is good that new ideas should be heard, for the sake of the few that can be used; but it is also good that new ideas should be compelled to go through the mill of objection, opposition and contumely; this is the trial heat which innovations must survive before being allowed to enter the human race. It is good that the old should resist the young, and that the young should prod the old; out of this tension, as out of the strife of the sexes and the classes, comes a creative tensile strength, a stimulated development, a secret and basic unity and movement of the whole.

THE ABOVE QUOTE appears in Will and Ariel Durant's book *The Lessons of History*, a small volume completed after their monumental ten-volume series, *The Story of Civilization*. It is a brief description of a healthy give-and-take in a utopian society, one that hardly ever, except in a given moment, exists in actual history. While I believe their description to be worth striving for, it seems to me there are undercurrents in most social situations that alter and affect the basic dynamics that the Durants describe. My case offers specific examples of how undercurrents subverted movement toward strength and wholeness and bypassed opportunities for creative tension.

The first undercurrent is of a very personal nature. I have been married three times—each time with the church's consent and in compliance with its canons. Some have suggested this may have made me seem to be a convenient and easy target. From 1946 to 1973, the church had a canon covering the possibility of remarriage after divorce. This canon was hopelessly inhumane, unrealistic, and one that encouraged dishonesty of the worst kind. Its administration depended upon the particular bishop's personal point of view in interpreting it and also on the point of view of the bishop's legal adviser, usually his chancellor. Everything hinged on whether the person wishing to remarry after a divorce had had a Christian marriage, a subject open to wide interpretation. Some bishops were known for saying that a divorce meant the Christian marriage had failed and therefore that the persons involved deserved a chance to have a new marriage. They asked that the parish priest, as the pastor for the couple, make sure that everyone involved was being honest. Other bishops delegated no authority and simply expected the priest to be the person who helped write the description of the situation. They made a distinction between a priori causes for the divorce (those that existed before the marriage occurred) and a posteriori causes (those that arose after the marriage occurred). A posteriori causes, these bishops felt, could be dealt with by the couple by means of medical and psychological assistance. A priori causes represented something akin to fraud and this kind of marriage could be called non-Christian. (And at least one of the parties involved could be given permission to marry another time.)

It was a minefield, complicated even more by the demeaning way in which the person who sought permission to remarry after divorce was treated by the bishop on behalf of the institution of the church. He or she was expected to wait a year from the final date of the divorce decree until the remarriage, no matter how long it had taken to get the decree. The parish priest, who, most of the time, wanted to be helpful, had to help the couple develop an a priori case, present it to the bishop, and then wait. Sometimes it took months to get an answer. Frequently, the bishop wanted to meet with the couple who wished to marry. Then the bishop had to consult with his chancellor. And finally an answer would come. No matter what the papers said, severe injustices were committed in enough cases over a period of time that by 1973 a new canon was produced.

In 1973, the Committee on Pastoral Development, chaired by the Bishop of Rochester, Robert Spears, offered a new canon. I had just arrived (in 1972) in the House of Bishops and was assigned to the committee. I found it almost exhilarating to be in on the committee's work. As a priest for twenty-one years before being elected to the episcopate, I found the previous canons unworkable, even though both the Bishop of Pittsburgh, Austin Pardue, and the Bishop of New Hampshire, Tod Hall, tried to put a humane face on them.

The canon that was adopted in 1973 by the General Convention meeting in Louisville, Kentucky, changed the emphasis. No longer did the couple have to seek the bishop's permission to remarry. No longer did they have to wait a year from the date of the divorce to remarry. No longer did they have to wrestle with a priori or a posteriori concepts. The couple was expected to consult with their parish priest. If the priest thought they should be permitted to remarry, it was the priest's responsibility to ask the bishop for permission to solemnize the ceremony. It was so straightforward and so just, it was almost miraculous in clearing the air.

Then the bishops went to work on the application of the canon. Some bishops still required the couple to apply to their bishop for permission to remarry. One bishop I know required thirty pages of paperwork to be filled out by the couple before he would even consider the possibility of their remarriage. Some bishops insisted that each couple wait a year before applying for permission to remarry, even though the canon did not require this. And, so far as I knew, clergy did not object. I suspect that many clergy did not even read the canon involved. Couples, I suspect, did not read it, either. They were seeking permission to remarry. They trusted their priest and their bishop to tell them what hoops they needed to jump through in order to achieve their goal. Injustice and insensitivity continued to exist under a blanket of Christian charity because of the way some bishops and some clergy were acting. In some dioceses, the language of the canon was taken seriously and acted upon appropriately.

Clergy were considered to be different. No matter how humane the marriage canon was meant to be, I found, in all my years as a parish priest, that if a priest got a divorce, he was forced to renounce his orders. No canon said he must, but no work would be available to him. I, who had lived through a marriage that was dying on the vine, knew this. I also knew that people of the church could not have cared less. I was expected to work seventy-hour weeks, maintaining the highest standards. But the institution showed little concern for my personal happiness and well-being and that of my wife and children. The bishop's chair that used to be used at St. James Church, Keene, New Hampshire, has carved into it in large letters BISHOPS SHALL BE BLAMELESS. It was representative of years and years when clergy were considered perfect. It is a healthy thing for the church that that image has been shattered.

The whole attitude toward divorce illustrates what can happen when the church tries to institute a change. The bishops who insisted on seeing the couple, who insisted on reams of paperwork, and who continued to insist upon a year's waiting period were hanging on to useless and outdated concepts. They were not dealing with the reality of divorce and remarriage and they were like King Canute standing on the beach, trying to hold back the tide. It did not work. In many cases, I suspect, there were both clergy and bishops holding very shaky marriages together, thinking that they couldn't hold their own situation together if they followed the new, more humane canon. It would have been healthier to face up to the situation, but the institution made that reality dangerous.

In Iowa, I met with all our clergy at a three-day clergy conference after the new canon on remarriage was adopted, and we discussed all the decisions the 1973 General Convention had made. When it came to the canon on marriage and remarriage, the clergy seemed to feel it was a step forward to be given the responsibility for determining if a marriage could occur. They were quite willing and pleased to be the people who asked the bishop for permission to solemnize the ceremony, instead of needing to hassle people about making a trip to Des Moines to see me. I suggested, in pragmatic terms, that they simply write me a letter asking for permission to officiate at the wedding of A and B. I said I would trust them and grant permission, unless they told me that they did not think the wedding should occur and they would like me to say no. For sixteen years, that system worked well. Only once in that period of time did anyone ask me to say no.

When the canon was administered fairly, no longer did clergy have to renounce their orders if they got a divorce. By dealing carefully with the people in their parishes and not asking them to take sides in the situation with their respective spouses, they were able to stay in the parish and continue their effective ministries, even when they felt compelled to seek a dissolution of their marriages. After about ten years of the existence of this canon, almost a third of the clergy in the Diocese of Iowa were people whose marriages had been dissolved. They had been able to face reality and to do so with the support of the bishop and the church. Most of them had remarried. Most of them were better clergy for having come to terms with impossible situations. Occasionally, they might make a mistake in their second marriage, as I did. If that happened, and they sought a divorce a second time, as I did, they were still able to continue with their parish duties. Perhaps they married a third time. The canon permitted that. It also asked that the pastoral ministry of the church be called upon much more clearly than the legalistic machinery. It expressed the truth that the church is meant to be a community of grace, rather than a community of law.

I have written the above to provide a context for one of the undercurrents; my own journey through two failed marriages was both personally painful and perhaps created a vulnerability my accusers seized upon. Clearly, my life has been different from that of the average bishop in the Episcopal Church who has not experienced and dealt with the distress and emotional and psychological pain of divorce personally, let alone the jarring impact that has on one's sacramental theology. To stand before a judge and say "Yes" to

"Has this marriage failed beyond repair?" is to admit to failure in a monumental way. That one-word answer really shook me when I gave it. Both Nancy and I were made to feel that instituting divorce proceedings was akin to flunking a sacrament, though both of us struggled for years to make those marriages work and paid a high psychic and emotional price in the process. While no one directly brought up my marriages during the presentment process, I felt it was there as a subtext.

While we have adopted on paper a very humane and honest way of being pastoral about remarriage after divorce, our leaders, and indeed our church culture, are still uneasy with it. I know countless people, joyful and grateful participants in marriages that have occurred "in church" as a result of our 1973 changes, who would say prayers of thanksgiving that the change occurred. I know countless others whose marriages occurred "in church" in spite of the previous system who would say about the 1973 change, "It's about time!" In spite of the previous system, and not at all because of it, there are faithful people who stuck it out. Their numbers are legion. The newer bishops who are being elected now do not have nearly as much of a historical residue, and, I trust, have formed more solid marriages than mine were. We have some important work to do to keep divorce humane, even as we protect children. We have a lot of work to do to plumb the depths of the experience of men and women who have gone through divorce, have remarried, and have a solid relationship now that has lasted for many years.

A second undercurrent present, if veiled, in my presentment was confusion about what could be called "family values." There is no question that the shape of the family has changed subtly but thoroughly in our time. For some people in love with the past, that change is unrecognizable. They cannot restore in reality what they hold on to as an ideal. Frankly, it never existed! But the family is still a significant entity in our society. Jane Howard, a writer who crisscrossed this country for almost a year in the 1970s, visiting with rich people, poor people, middle-class people, double-parent families, single-parent families, gay or lesbian families, black families, white families, and families of mixed marriages, concluded that the family is as strong as it ever was and in some ways even stronger. Its structure is simply more varied than it has been in the past. To trumpet "family values" as right-wing conservatives have done in the past decade is to reduce this great variety and diversity to simplistic definitions: A family exists when there is a male parent and a female parent. Not so, says Howard. Not so, says the experience of a vast number of Americans. The Episcopal Church is just beginning to recognize the necessity for its ministry to single-parent families, gay-parent families, and childless families. To which I say, "Alleluia!"

We are in the midst of a vast struggle about permitting people in same-sex marriages to have their relationship blessed. Barry Stopfel and Will Leckie are a family. Anyone who knows them and has spent time with them in their home can see the obvious. In Barry's parish, there are same-sex couples with children they have adopted. They are families. Many young couples in heterosexual marriages have sought an inclusive parish. They have found it at St. George's! Many so-called traditional families may share a house together, but the sense of love and compassion and forgiveness is absent. Nancy and I know all too well the pain and the emotional numbness that comes of living that lie.

In his 1997 Easter message, the Archbishop of Canterbury said that couples living together without benefit of marriage "will bring down the institution of marriage." To me, that seems an oversimplification that makes no reference to the dynamics of relationships. I see no reason for strong marriages to be undone by the commitments of other couples. But the Archbishop of Canterbury's statement is clearly illustrative of the limited mind-set that exists among many of the leaders of our church. Surely some of this rigidity about marriage and "family values" played itself out in the minds of the bishops who signed my presentment and who voted for a trial.

Perhaps the most fundamental undercurrent registering in my presentment was the apprehension that accompanies rapid change in every aspect of life. Sometimes it seems to be coming at us like a giant wave. Tod Hall, the Bishop of New Hampshire during my seventeen years in Nashua, spoke many times about the role of faith as it tries to "make sense out of the nonsense of life." In part because of the accelerated pace of change, individuals, institutions, and faith communities have had difficulty keeping up with change and adjusting to it.

One area of life where new developments have outpaced understanding is the arena of human sexuality. The constructs that once helped us make sense of sexual relationships are no longer useful. For example, women were for long periods of Euro-American history considered to be the property of men. Gradually, that idea has changed, yet many of the remnants of women's subordination to men resurrect themselves in discussions of divorce, the ordination of women, and the delegation of authority to women.

Touching any sexual issue today is like touching a bowl of Jell-O. You push in one place and it wobbles all over. Issues of birth control, abortion, homosexuality, and spousal and clerical abuse stir anxiety, resistance, and even hot denial.

In the early 1990s, the Presbyterian church produced a report, issued from a group within the church called the

Special Committee on Human Sexuality, that grappled with many of these issues. They argued that "fidelity makes relationships of durability, substance, and hope possible"; "a reformed Christian ethic of sexuality will not condemn, out of hand, any sexual relations in which there is genuine equality and mutual respect"; "we are persuaded that the fundamental debate within the church, as well as in society, should not be focused in a limited way on rules about who sleeps with whom—we should be asking whether the relationship is responsible, the dynamics genuinely mutual and the loving full of caring." Sadly, at the Presbyterian General Assembly, the report was turned down; instead, the General Assembly affirmed the sanctity of marriage, a way of conveying this message: "We will not permit same-sex unions."

In recent years, this discussion has been played out in all the major religious groups in the United States: the National Conference of Catholic Bishops, the United Methodist church, the Episcopal Church, the United Church of Christ, Judaism—and it certainly played a significant role in defining the confusion, anger, and defensiveness behind and beneath my presentment.

In a graduation address given by the Rev. Charles Price at Virginia Theological Seminary in 1989, he suggested that "the liberal tradition of the Gospel and the conservative tradition of the Gospel are not necessarily antithetical, although they are often perceived so." Echoing the Durants' notion of "creative tension," he reminds us that the Gospel is a humane, tolerant, skeptical, and ultimately liberating tradition.

During the presentment process, there were times when I think we lost sight of that balance, that creative dynamic. An accusation invites black/white, win/lose thinking. In my case being cited for trial for heresy raised questions about the church's view of the permanence of marriage, the meaning of the sacraments, the meaning of family values—the whole range of human sexuality. I am not so naïve as to think that these questions have been dispatched, or that my side has "won." Rather, I pray that in our struggles we may strive to bring forth, in the words of Will and Ariel Durant, "a creative tensile strength, a stimulated development, a secret and basic unity and movement of the whole."

CHAPTER 9

Full Circle

THE GENERAL CONVENTION of the Episcopal Church is a triennial adventure for more than a thousand official representatives of their dioceses and for several thousand additional persons officially classed as visitors. The Episcopal Church Women (ECW) meets at the same time and place, adding a few thousand more to the official representatives and visitors. I have been told that we are the third-largest convention to meet regularly in the United States, nosed out in size only by the Republican and Democratic nominating conventions, which meet every four years. The gathering provides an important opportunity for maintaining relationships and nurturing friendships. Those reunions are so numerous that one conventiongoer said, "A convention is a meeting where no one ever finishes a sentence."

Both Nancy and I realized how stressful the 1997 convention would be for us, because we attended a preconvention meeting for bishops and delegates from Province I (the New England dioceses) held in Holyoke, Massachusetts, that May.

Its aim was to acquaint us with some of the legislation we were going to be considering at the July General Convention. It did that, but it also alerted us to the strength of our feelings about some of the issues. Not infrequently, as these issues were discussed, the "Righter case" was used as a point of reference. Since my presence was never acknowledged, I felt like a thing instead of a person. Once again, I was reminded of those accusers who kept saying to me, "Don't take this personally" and who tried to dehumanize the process of a heresy trial. Nancy and I continued to put a human face on the process we had endured, so the Holyoke meeting, with its impersonal references, felt hauntingly familiar and distressing.

Not only did "the Righter case" supersede the actual presence of Walter and Nancy Righter; we also discovered how thoroughly hierarchical a church ours is. Nancy tried to speak as a layperson to some of the proposals, but she found it hard to be recognized, in spite of holding her hand up high. When she was recognized, little was done with her remarks. Lay opinion is not easily noticed or, apparently, effectively integrated into the discussion.

A note of humor that was not intended did brighten the day for us. The leader of one session we were sitting in on referred to "the Righter case" and the "woman" whom I had ordained to the diaconate! Gene Robinson, executive secretary of the province, saw us afterward and, with a big grin on his face, said, "I can't wait to tell Barry he is a woman!" The Holyoke meeting didn't really alert us to new issues, but it did provide a dress rehearsal for the kinds of feelings we would experience when we got to Philadelphia for the General Convention.

A month before the convention, I was invited to speak at a luncheon meeting at a manufacturing plant in Massachusetts. The corporation that owns the plant is Lucent Technologies. Lucent sponsors an organization for its gay and lesbian employees called Equal, whose planning and presentation is very professional. I was invited to speak about my experience of being accused of heresy in the Episcopal Church. Company policy insists that Lucent employees take training in understanding and appreciating diversity. One of the company executives, who was present at the meeting the day I spoke, told me the executives have accepted a discipline among themselves, agreeing to challenge anyone who does not honor diversity and support it. The discussion we had, while we were eating, made it quite clear that there is a real commitment in that company to recognize a social phenomenon and act upon it. Would that our bishops could embrace such an attitude.

The weekend before going off to Philadelphia, Nancy and I were the leaders of a workshop at the national convention of Dignity, the Roman Catholic organization for gays and lesbians, equivalent to Integrity in the Episcopal Church. The theme of the convention was "We are called Prophets to the World," and the workshops focused on how each person is called to be a prophet. We attended a banquet on Saturday evening where awards of merit were given to members who had done unusual service for the gay and lesbian cause. The banquet was accompanied by a dance where gay and lesbian couples were free to dance with one another, hold hands with one another, and be affectionate with one another. A breath of fresh air, it was a symbol of the kingdom we all hoped for— freedom to express and live out healthy, wholesome relationships. The following day, a Sunday morning, we led our workshop and were each given a stole as a symbol of our roles as prophets. Each attendee was given a stole. Nancy and I felt quite honored to be included. Like our attendance at the

Holyoke meeting, this, too, helped us prepare for Philadelphia. Our natural community, supportive and unconditionally loving, was the community of persons in any church concerned with peace and justice issues. Holyoke had taught us how sensitive our feelings about the events of the last two years were; Lucent Technology showed how the corporate world could respond sensitively to social issues; and the Dignity convention reaffirmed how significant it is to be with a community of persons who share your convictions. All would be a part of our experience in Philadelphia.

The scenes in Philadelphia were familiar to me. From a distance, I saw the City Hall, with, as my grandfather used to say, "Billy Penn on top." It was the tallest building in the city when I was a child, and the statue of William Penn was so huge that it was said you could drive a horse and wagon around William Penn's hat brim. Now that tall building is surrounded by newer, taller buildings, the familiar surrounded by the unfamiliar. Intellectually, I understood it. Emotionally, it took some getting used to. Reading Station, a railroad station very familiar to me as a youngster, now has on the street floor restaurants and shops with a potpourri of food choices.

The hotel where we were to stay was another surprise. It was built on a spot where a small department store had been at a time when Philadelphia had more than a handful of department stores and before the suburbs became the shopping meccas they were after World War II. We registered, found our room, and went in search of the registration desk for the General Convention. Once more, I found the familiar in the midst of the unfamiliar. We walked through an enclosed passageway from the hotel into the Philadelphia Convention Center. It was huge! It seemed familiar, but I did not know why. When a passerby reminded us that we were walking on railroad rails that had been enclosed in a marble floor, I recognized another railroad station that I had often run through as a child. I conjectured, Maybe those rails were made in the steel mill my grandfather managed for American Bridge! Within a few minutes, we found the registration desk and our participation in the General Convention of 1997 began.

Before going to the convention, I changed the license plate on my car to HRETIC, never passing up an opportunity to poke fun at the whole thing. When we got there and registered, my name tag clearly named me as "Assisting Bishop, Newark." Since I am canonically resident in Iowa, it was changed to read "Iowa, Retired." Nancy's said "Alstead, NH, Visitor"—hardly descriptive of her life in the church. When asked by a convention volunteer if she wanted it to read "Iowa," she declined and playfully asked if it could read "Heretic's Wife." The reply was a smiling "You can have anything you want." After an hour of sharing that exchange with anyone who would listen, she realized she needed to change her badge. "Heretic's Wife" became a litmus test for a sense of humor and brought friendly laughter from many.

At every General Convention I have ever attended, including one in Philadelphia in 1946, there is a space for exhibits. There one can find vestments and books and jewelry to buy, information about insurance and pensions, and data from the many different groups representing points of view about the church's mission. The Consultation is a group of organizations that has banded together to advocate for the peace and justice ministries of the church. Their convention daily, *Issues,* is the liberal voice for the convention. This year, these organizations, Integrity, Episcopal Peace Fellowship, Women's Caucus, Union of Black Episcopalians, and urban and environmental groups, among others, were all in the same general area of the exhibit hall. Nancy found herself very much at home there and I did, too, when I was not sitting in the House of Bishops. All Saints Church, Pasadena, had a booth nearby, highlighting their theme of "Beyond Inclusion," as did *The Witness* magazine and Oasis. It was a welcoming area, and for Nancy, it became a home base when she needed to be restored.

Another welcoming area, although much less personal, was the area where we worshiped each day. Approximately three thousand people worshiped at a daily Eucharist, with the space arranged with tables, each seating ten persons. The priest at our table was Jim Simons of St. Michael's in the Valley, Rector, Pennsylvania, the church I started forty-eight years ago. Instead of a sermon after the reading of the Gospel each day, all at the table participated in a discussion of that Gospel's meaning for each one of us. The idea of gathering in small groups was a stroke of genius that began at Phoenix in 1991 after the bishops had experienced something like that at Lambeth Conference in 1988. It is, from my point of view, a fine way to assist people of all orders and all ages in sharing, deepening, and, at times, updating their faith.

The House of Bishops was less welcoming than either of the areas I have just described. I am certain that everyone was quite conscious of the fact that I was the first bishop accused, but not quite tried, to return to that House with full credentials. The House of Bishops, like the worship area, is arranged with tables, these for eight people each. Those at my table were Hunt Williams, retired Suffragan Bishop of North Carolina; O'Kelley Whitaker, retired Bishop of Central New York; Tom Ray, Bishop of Northern Michigan; and Jim Krotz, Bishop of Nebraska. All the additional space at the table was taken up by the books and papers needed in our legislative process. We began our time together with some sharing about what we had done since we last met. Everyone had a chance to talk except me, and I had only a few minutes before we were called back to order. I did have a chance to say I was finishing a book about my experience of being accused of heresy, but it seemed to make people slightly edgy to mention the presentment in any way. Avoidance wasn't a possibility for me; on the other hand, I was acutely conscious of the fact that ten of my fellow bishops had attempted to have me tried, and sixty-six additional members had voted in favor of doing that. The only other trial in the church's history had resulted in a bishop being deposed and never returning. Here I was, and there was a strangeness about being here. I had felt strangeness in my relationship with the House of Bishops in the past, but now the presentment continued to intrude into many of my encounters with people.

Beyond the House of Bishops, life seemed enormously busy as we immersed ourselves in the General Convention. There were special luncheons and dinners to attend, hearings on legislation to participate in, and special services and gatherings to attend between the dinners and the legislative hearings. The distance from hotel to convention seemed excessively long at times. The acoustics in the areas where the House of Deputies and the House of Bishops met were, for a person wearing a hearing aid, far from satisfactory. Almost as much energy as was spent on relationships was required to negotiate getting from place to place and trying to be attentive. We rose by 7:00 a.m. every day and seldom got back to our room before 9:00 p.m. Persons serving on committees put in even longer days. One afternoon, while Nancy volunteered at the NEAC (National Episcopal AIDS Coalition) booth, Steve Snider stole me away from the convention simply to get some relief from the intense process. We traveled in Lower Merion, Roxborough, Manayunk, and Wissahickon—areas in which my family had lived. There were so many places that were familiar, and I kept pointing them out, that Steve was led to observe that this area should truly be named "Righterville."

The 72d General Convention was an eerie experience for both of us. My presentment was rarely mentioned in discussions of official business, but its influence on attitudes and particular pieces of legislation was apparent everywhere. The spirit of the convention was more positive than any in my memory. As we moved through the halls of the convention, hundreds of people stopped us and thanked both of us for the witness we had borne during that fifteen-month period. At the end of each day, I found myself exhausted from meeting and talking with so many persons I had not met before, and from the excitement of renewing old friendships. Most encounters, while pleasant, were too short.

Some of the convention represented for both of us another emotional roller-coaster ride. The vote affirming the 1976 decision to ordain women and requiring each diocese to open the process leading to ordination to women as well as men was a high. The vote to turn down the development of a rite for blessing same-sex relationships by one vote was a deep disappointment for us. But for our friends in the gay and lesbian community there was rejoicing—we had lost by only one vote. The first really full day for us was the day we had normal worship and small group Bible study in the morning, followed before lunch with a legislative session. Then lunch and another legislative session in the afternoon. The evening was crammed, for some reason. We barely had time for a bite to eat, then off to a nearby church for the Integrity Eucharist, celebrated by Ed Browning, with a sermon by Elizabeth Kaeton, director of Oasis in the Diocese of Newark. Elizabeth ably connected our erotic side with the wholeness of the Christian faith, and Integrity had an opportunity to thank their Presiding Bishop for his faithfulness to them. Then off to testify at a hearing on the proposal to develop rites for blessing of same-sex relationships. It was tempting to think that someone had scheduled those two events back-to-back on purpose to make it more difficult for the gay and lesbian community to attend both.

Nancy and I each testified at the hearing on that legislation, but some of what we heard was troubling. There were at least fifty people speaking on behalf of each side, including laypersons, clergy, and bishops. Those testifying against the resolution were heavy with judgment against gay and lesbian people, liberally misusing the Bible to justify their prejudice. Those testifying for the resolution clearly saw it as a part of our mission and ministry. The fact that the resolution lost by only one vote means it will probably pass at the General Convention in the year 2000, but listening to hateful words spoken as "God's words" by those opposed was a painful experience.

The next day, we were up early in order for me to testify at a hearing against a resolution to take the vote away from retired bishops. This proposal has come up several times since I have been in the House of Bishops. Each time, it was defeated. This time, I had a very personal reason for wanting it defeated. Twice in the two-hundred-year history of the Episcopal Church there have been accusations against a bishop for heresy that have moved toward trial. Each time, the accused was a retired bishop. In view of that, it seemed wise to retain the vote for retired bishops. Nancy and I also did a statistical analysis of the votes to have a trial—25 percent needed. Exactly 25 percent of the active bishops voted for a trial. Exactly 25 percent of the retired bishops voted for a trial. Any penalty that is imposed as a result of a trial must have a two-thirds vote of the bishops before it can be carried out. It seemed wise to let the retired bishops keep the vote if they were the only ones who were going to be cited. The bishops voted to take the vote away. The House of Deputies voted against it. So retired bishops still vote.

During a break in our legislative process, Nancy and I stopped at the armed forces booth in the exhibit hall. Both of us, in spite of my service in World War II, are pacifists by nature. Nancy's son, David, has just finished his master's degree in kinesiology—exercise science. His research proved so superb that the army solicited him to join their research efforts in that field. After extensive interviewing, he agreed to enlist and continue his research under army auspices. It raised the whole question of pacifism in Nancy's mind, and we talked with the people in the armed forces booth extensively about it. We also came away with an armed forces cross for each of us and small prayer books for Dave and his wife, Maryrose. We put our crosses on our name tags, next to our pink triangles. It was a good experience for both of us to know about the Episcopal Church's ministry to the armed forces through such a personal encounter.

This General Convention was to be a particularly distinctive one because of the election of Ed Browning's successor as Presiding Bishop. After several days of speculation about candidates and much anticipation, we elected a native Pennsylvanian, Frank Griswold, who was, at the time of his election, the Bishop of Chicago. It is his responsibility to be our Presiding Bishop through 2006. But the retiring Presiding Bishop was a powerful and courageous voice at this convention. His farewell address to a joint session of the House of Deputies and the House of Bishops was gracious; he thanked people for the work they had been and are doing together, and stated his own convictions. He was interrupted by applause frequently, but two passages stand out in my mind. One concerns women: "I long ago reached the conclusion that God never intended that only half of the human race should run this world, or this church. . . . The ministry of women has brought a wholeness to our ministry. Our experience has been a model for other provinces in the Anglican Communion. . . ." The second concerns human sexuality: "We actually do agree on most issues around sexuality. We agree on the sanctity of marriage. We agree that exploitative relationships and abusive relationships are evil. We have a message for our culture about this. We should be delivering it with unity and strength. Instead we have been diverted by fear, and let me name it, by hate. . . . Some of the most extreme among us have used the disagreement within our body to foment difficulty and advance themselves and their causes. This is not of God."

Uniting these issues in his thanksgiving, he said, "I give thanks and praise for the women who have enriched the ordained ministry of this church. I give thanks and praise for our gay and lesbian brothers and sisters who serve this church so faithfully. I give thanks and praise to all people of color in this church, who make us so much more a reflection of God's creation."

Perhaps most important, Browning spoke out strongly on the subject of Scripture and its interpretation:

As Anglicans, we discern God's will through Scripture, tradition, and reason. However, some have chosen to embrace biblical literalism instead of our Anglican tradition. History tells us that biblical literalism was used to support both the practice of slavery and the denigration of women. We have moved past slavery and we are moving past the oppression of women. It is time to move past using literalistic readings of the Bible to create prejudices against our gay and lesbian brothers and sisters. Biblical literalism may be someone's tradition, but it's not our tradition, and it's time we came home to our Anglican roots.

Some of those present—some of my accusers among them—were upset by these words, but for most of us, it was a joy to hear this strong endorsement of the Anglican tradition of biblical interpretation from our Presiding Bishop. More exciting things happened. As previously noted, the House of Deputies passed overwhelmingly the resolution making it mandatory for each diocese to allow women access to the process leading toward ordination, and to allow women to be licensed in each diocese. This same motion passed in the House of Bishops as well, by a substantial majority. Bishops whose consciences will not permit them to ordain women may still abstain from ordaining them. But they are not allowed to institutionalize their consciences by imposing their own personal point of view on the structures, committees, and commissions of their dioceses. Nor are bishops allowed to deny a woman a job in their diocese simply because she is a woman. If a parish wants to call a woman rector, or a priest in that diocese wants a woman assistant, the bishop is now required to permit that to happen. There was some effort on the part of the four bishops who will not ordain women to transfer to a nearby diocese any parish desiring the ministry of a woman priest. That simply did not wash! A bishop needs to, at the very least, permit the diocese he or she serves to follow the will of the General Convention.

During the debate about this action, there was an ironic twist. The four bishops refusing to ordain women, all presenters against me, tried to have a resolution passed exempting them from any presentment in the next three years. Many in the House of Bishops spoke to me about that—some in dismay, some in anger. Neither emotion was expressed in public debate. The legislative process itself, including the public debate, contained and controlled such a willful attempt to permit a few people to disregard the action of the General Convention. There were no public acrimonious comments, but there was no question that the House of Bishops would not permit that kind of exemption to occur. By not accepting the proposal, which came in the form of an amendment to the resolution about the ordination of women, it was dealt with legislatively. The amendment failed. The resolution passed without any watering down of its intent. At last, 50 percent of the world's population is now definitively included in those who can seek ordination in the Episcopal Church. That was voted, clearly, in 1976, but after twenty-one years, we needed to reaffirm that clarity. The irony is obvious. The ten people who presented (accused) me of heresy, made that accusation on the basis of General Convention resolutions. Four of the ten, who still refuse to permit women access to the process leading to ordination, are in violation of the canons of the church. They have created a strange "through the looking glass" world—resolutions that must be obeyed, canons that are optional!

I sat quietly through all this debate, not saying anything, not debating, but bubbling and boiling in my own way. And I was very pleased with the clear statement that the vote represented.

More clarity occurred, as well. Gay and lesbian persons are much more visibly in the mainstream of the life of the Episcopal Church than they have been in the past, although not completely so. Health benefits for domestic partners of clergy and church employees were approved, if requested by a diocese. Pension benefits for surviving partners were not approved. While a resolution authorizing the development of liturgies for blessings of same-sex committed relationships was defeated by one vote in the House of Deputies, another resolution calling for the continued theological study of blessings by the Standing Commission on Common Worship was passed by both Houses. And a report is to be made available with recommended future steps by November 1999 for consideration by the next General Convention, to be held in the year 2000.

A significant resolution, which began in the House of Deputies and passed on the final day in both Houses, stated that "while acknowledging the diversity of opinion among the Bishops and deputies of this Convention on the morality of gay and lesbian sexual relationships, this 72d General Convention apologizes on behalf of the Episcopal Church to its members who are gay or lesbian and to lesbians and gay men outside the church for years of rejection and maltreatment by the church."

My hope and prayer is that the church is awakening to the importance of, as well as the existence of, diversity. At the very least, the agenda of the gay and lesbian community was openly discussed at the General Convention. Some of the desired legislation lost. But much legislation that was not only desired but also needed for the sake of justice was passed. History was made. The place of gay and lesbian people in the life of the Episcopal Church was not only declared by the Presiding Bishop in his address; it became rooted in our life through legislative action. Gay and lesbian people were visible as responsible delegates caring profoundly about the agendas of others as well as their own.

On Friday evening, another milestone was passed. We attended the *Witness* dinner and took part in a program that gave awards to Leon Modeste, Coleman McGehee, Verna Dozier, and the Ojibwe Singers. The awards, given in the name of William Scarlett, deceased Bishop of Missouri; William Spofford, longtime *Witness* editor; William Stringfellow, lawyer and thinker of great clarity about powers and principalities; and Vida Scudder, churchwoman and socialist, recognize activity that is outstanding and transforming in our society. It was an honor to be present and witness the awards and hear the recipients respond. Paul Washington, retired rector of the Church of the Advocate, where the dinner was held, was recognized informally. It was in this church where the first ordination of women occurred in 1974. Paul, as the rector of the church, was an outstanding leader, especially in the development of the General Convention Special Program, which Leon Modeste directed, in the era of Presiding Bishop John Hines. It was a steamy, hot evening. Huge fans in the church only increased the noise level. But the sound I heard above all else was the sound of a church working to cross frontiers, working to enfranchise all of her children.

A highlight of the time in Philadelphia for us was the Integrity Convention Luncheon, to which we were invited as speakers. Fred Ellis, the national president of Integrity, presented to each of us a beautiful certificate, of the Louie Crew Award, for "distinguished lesbian and gay ministry in the Episcopal Church." We consider it a great honor to be placed in association with our dear friend Louie.

Much of the positive spirit of this convention is, I think, evidence of a backlash against my presentment, a recognition that accusing a retired bishop of heresy has little to do with the mission and ministry of the church. Negativism has lost its attractiveness. There was, and I believe still is, a groundswell among the leaders of this church in local congregations that says simply, "Let's get with it!" That, it seems to me, is an indirect fallout from the presentment.

Beyond that observable shift in attitude, there were some things at this convention that were direct results of the Righter presentment. Two examples occurred in resolutions that attempted a clearer definition of what constitutes doctrine and discipline in the Episcopal Church. The Court for the Trial of a Bishop concluded that I had violated no "core doctrine," and no "core discipline," but apart from the arguments of my attorney, there was no clear definition of either. These resolutions attempted to correct that. The first resolution located the discipline of the church in "the Constitution, the Canons, and the rubrics and ordinal of the Book of Common Prayer." The second defined doctrine as the basic and essential teachings of the church found in the canons of Holy Scripture as understood in the Apostles' and Nicene creeds and in the sacramental rites, ordinal, and catechism in the Book of Common Prayer.

When my accusers announced that they would not appeal the decision of the court, they appropriated a much narrower definition of discipline and doctrine. They said, "The only appeal of this case that will be taken is an appeal to those who accept the authority of the Holy Scriptures of the Old and New Testaments in the sense indicated by the author of II Timothy 3:16–17," which reads as follows: "All scripture is inspired by God and is useful for teaching, for reproof, for correction, and for training in righteousness, so that everyone who belongs to God may be proficient, equipped for every good work" (NRSV). Since those verses were written, and since the formation and the spread of the Christian church, a significant proviso must be added. The church is a living, protean, evolving entity. It is the church that decides which books are included in the Bible. It is the church that decides what the meaning of the verses and the books really is. It is the church's task to interpret that meaning continually and not simply to accept the words as they are printed in English in a particular translation of the Greek and Hebrew texts. It is not unusual for a person who is accustomed to a literalistic interpretation and use of the Bible to become a member of the Episcopal Church. They join a church that uses and interprets God's word in a nonliteral manner. They are accepted as persons. They embrace our way of life even as they are being embraced by this, our community of faith. Currently, at least one seminary teaches the literal use of Scripture, and some clergy and bishops make literal use of Scripture, yet the basic Episcopal tradition has not altered.

Gay and lesbian people are created by God. To honor that creation is our task. To do that as an institution representing God's mission and purpose in the world may be slow, but it must be steady. At times, the institution may seem to be like a small child who does not want to be moved and becomes deadweight. History has similar inert moments, moments of deadweight, and stasis. How long did it take for the institutions of the world to move from believing the "flat earth" theory to accepting the "round earth" theory? How long did it take to accept the truth that the earth was not the center of the universe? It took only a short time for Galileo to be excommunicated from the Roman Catholic church, but some four hundred years for him to be reinstated. How many years did it take for at least part of the world to get rid of the idea of slavery as a part of God's plan? How long did it take to say women could be ordained in the Episcopal Church? And how long have gay and lesbian people had to suffer rejection, mistreatment, and abuse? In each of the above instances, it was and is clear what God has created. In each instance, institutions have behaved like a recalcitrant child, and then finally they have given in and walked forward again.

On one of our last evenings in Philadelphia, we attended a healing service held by the National Episcopal AIDS Coalition (NEAC). Ted Karpf, then executive director of NEAC, had asked all candidates for Presiding Bishop, long before the election of Frank Griswold, if they would come to that service and participate in the laying on of hands and the healing prayers. Three of them did—Frank Griswold, Richard Shimpfky, and Herb Thompson. When the service ended, we were headed to our Province I dinner, too far to walk. As we started looking for a taxi, Ted said, "Go get in the van!" and he pointed to it. Then he yelled to the driver, "Take Walter and Nancy." As we climbed into the van, we found ourselves riding with Presiding Bishop-Elect Frank Griswold and his wife, Phoebe, and Pam Chinnis, president of the House of Deputies. We had not formally met Phoebe, but our brief ride was delightful. Frank's excitement about his future task was obvious. Pam had been elected to another term as president of the House of Deputies and was looking forward to that. Phoebe was a welcoming presence and a very genuine-seeming person. Like all encounters at the convention, it was brief, personal, and filled with promise.

Whenever you do your best, as the Episcopal Church did at this convention, there are those who do not like what you do. The action on the ordination of women and the action with respect to gays and lesbians provoked the Episcopal Synod of America, representing approximately 1 percent of Episcopalians, to issue an open letter saying it would further its work "on a new province, a structure which would proclaim true doctrine and allow us to go forward with the work God has given each of us." In their attacks on the actions of the General Convention, the ESA was joined by the American Anglican Council, whose leader is Jim Stanton, Bishop of Dallas, Texas, one of my accusers. The Synod called for a registry of all clergy ordained by female bishops, because in the eyes of the Synod people, those ordinations are not valid. A friend who is a YMCA director once told me, "If you please fifty percent of the people fifty percent of the time you are doing a one hundred percent job!"

Less than a month after the convention, the American Psychological Association passed overwhelmingly a resolution that asserts there is no sound scientific evidence of the efficacy of what are called "reparative therapies." Such therapy, represented at the General Convention by a booth in the exhibit hall, claims the ability to change sexual orientation, although the use of the word *orientation* is not allowed. We now have scientific literature to back up what we have felt all along—our sexuality, in all its forms, is a gift from God, not to be manipulated or distorted after our creation at birth.

Heading home to New Hampshire from Philadelphia, both Nancy and I had a sense of completeness and closure. We had attended our Presiding Bishop's retirement banquet and the festive evening afterward. I participated in the election of a new Presiding Bishop. There was a completeness about both of those events. We were honored by Integrity, a community that has been for us a constant example of unconditional love. The actions of this convention had, for the most part, been positive ones for both peace and justice, especially the need for us to be an inclusive church, honoring our baptismal promise to "respect the dignity of every human being." There was a sense, as we drove farther and farther toward home, that the tensions of the past two and a half years were slipping away. So many old friends and as many new friends had thanked us for what we had done that we were certain there had not only been closure to our own ordeal but also closure to this time of mean-spiritedness in the church. Tentatively, we have returned to a sense of mission and ministry. Carefully, we have adopted a budget that is realistic. The treasurer of the church, Steve Duggan, said, "We stopped the bleeding." Now let us get on with the mission.

Something new in the life of the church has begun. To borrow from the name of a conference held at All Saints Church, Pasadena, in the spring of 1997, we have begun to go beyond inclusion. It is through the ministry of parish churches throughout the country—such as All Saints, Pasadena; All Saints, Brookline, Massachusetts; St. Paul's Cathedral in San Diego; All Saints, Hoboken, and St. George's, Maplewood, in New Jersey—that we have a sense that the cause for which we stand is no longer isolated to only one or two dioceses or to Integrity. The cause for justice, for inclusivity for all God's children, is rooted in the life of the Episcopal Church in the United States. The church is back on track. And we are back in New Hampshire, to our house in the hills and woods, to our golden retriever, to a clearer realization and deeper appreciation of "the peace of God, which passeth all understanding." I said to a friend upon returning and debriefing the experience with him, "Well, I don't know what I'll do now!" He looked at me with one eyebrow cocked and said, "You'll find an adventure, I'm sure!"

In truth, I would like to be ordained right now rather than retiring. There is a new spirit stirring, one that promises to make the next fifty years far more exciting and effective ones for the Christian faith. Both laypersons and ordained persons face unusual possibilities for ministry. A pilgrim's way always contains its moments of hesitation—even of full stop—before it accelerates once again. I am glad my journey has been a part of that "immense journey," one taking us into the new millennium.

A NOTE ABOUT THE AUTHOR

Walter Cameron Righter was born in Philadelphia in 1923. Following military service in World War II, he received his B.A. from the University of Pittsburgh in 1948 and his M.Div. from the Berkeley Divinity School in 1951. After ordination in the Episcopal Church, he served churches in Aliquippa and Georgetown, Pennsylvania, and Nashua, New Hampshire. He was consecrated Bishop of Iowa in 1972 and held that post through 1988. Following retirement, he served as interim rector at churches in Rockford, Illinois, and Ridgewood, New Jersey, and as an assisting bishop in the Diocese of Newark from 1989 to 1991. He and his wife now live in Alstead, New Hampshire.

A NOTE ON THE TYPE

The text of this book was set in Ehrhardt, a typeface based on the specimens of "Dutch" types found at the Ehrhardt foundry in Leipzig. The original design of the face was the work of Nicholas Kis, a Hungarian punch cutter known to have worked in Amsterdam from 1680 to 1689. The modern version of Ehrhardt was cut by the Monotype Corporation of London in 1937.

Composed by Creative Graphics, Allentown, Pennsylvania
Printed and bound by The Haddon Craftsmen,
an R.R. Donnelley & Sons Company, Bloomsburg, Pennsylvania
Designed by Robert C. Olsson